WILDFLOWERS OF THE ADIRONDACKS

by
Anne McGrath

with

Joanne Treffs

NORTH COUNTRY BOOKS
Sylvan Beach, N.Y. 13157

Printed and bound by Canterbury Press, Rome, New York

CONTENTS

ACKNOWLEDGMENTS

Nancy C. Olmstead, former Research Associate, Connecticut Arboretum and co-author of *The Audubon Society Field Guide to North American Wildflowers*, Eastern Region has been extremely helpful in the preparation of this book. Her advice, suggestions and time spent in correcting the text are greatly appreciated.

Our deepest thanks also go to those persons, dear to each of us, who gave help, encouragement, love and support at all times.

Anne McGrath
Joanne Treffs

INTRODUCTION

This book is a field guide to the most common and conspicuous wild flowers found in the Adirondack area, but not restricted to it. Our purpose in presenting a regional guide is to make identification of the local flora easier and quicker for the non-botanist by including only those species which grow here.

The only wild flower book illustrated with photographs that is currently available for this region, it contains descriptions and photographs of 120 species, representing 45 families. Several vines and shrubs have been included because of their showy blossoms, and an additional 51 flowers have been discussed in the text.

Although all of the pictures were taken within the Adirondack Park, most of the same flowers can be found in northern Vermont, New Hampshire and Maine. Many of them, except for a few high altitude plants, can also be found in the lowlands of New York and New England. The book, therefore, will be useful throughout all of the North Country as well as the surrounding countryside.

Anne McGrath

ARRANGEMENT OF BOOK

The descriptions and photographs in this book have been arranged very simply with flowers grouped first by color and then by time of bloom, from earliest to latest, within each color group. In the text this information is given in the upper right hand corner of each description, making it easy for you to select quickly the appropriate section where you are likely to find your flower described.

Sometimes a species will produce flowers in more than one color; in this case the major color will be listed first and the others will follow, i.e. WHITE/PINK/LAVENDER. If, however, you see a hyphenated color, such as RED-YELLOW, it indicates a red and yellow flower, not red flowers and yellow flowers. Because color variations often occur within a species, it may occasionally be necessary to look in a closely related color group to locate your flower.

The dates for flowering given beneath the color designation in the text and under each photograph are approximate only. Do not be surprised to find variations from what is given here. Climate and environment often produce extremes. This is true also for size.

You will find that the order of the descriptive material is uniform. Under the heading which gives the common and botanical names for the plant and the family to which it belongs, the flower size and plant height are given. A word of caution here, sometimes a cluster of tiny flowers may be mistaken for a single flower and you will have to look closely to see individual blossoms. Queen Anne's Lace is an example of this. In the body of the text, the first paragraph describes the flower, the leaves, and other parts of the plant when significant. The second paragraph tells where the plant grows and may also include such information as other common names for it, comparisons with other species, and some remarks on its history or use.

The photographs are presented in the same order as the text descriptions. Page and plate numbers will lead you from one to the other.

The scientific names used follow *Gray's Manual of Botany*, 8th ed. by Merritt Lyndon Fernald, and *Wild Flowers of the United States*, Vol. 2, by H. W. Rickett. The common names are from various sources. *The Audubon Society Field Guide to North American Wildflowers*, William A. Niering and Nancy C. Olmstead, *A Field Guide to Wildflowers*, Roger Tory Peterson and Margaret McKenney, and *Newcomb's Wildflower Guide*, Lawrence Newcomb, were also consulted when preparing this work.

We have mentioned in this book several flowers that should never be picked because they are becoming rare. In New York State these flowers and a number of others are protected by law. For a complete list you can write to the New York State Department of Environmental Conservation, 50 Wolf Rd., Albany, N.Y. 12233.

GLOSSARY

Achene
: A small dry fruit containing one seed and covered by a thin wall that does not burst open when ripe.

Alpine
: The open area above the treeline.

Alternate leaves
: Leaves placed singly on the stem, not opposite.

Annual
: A plant that lives for only one season or year.

Anther
: That part of the stamen that contains the pollen.

Axil
: The upper side of the angle formed where the leaf joins the stem.

Basal leaves
: The leaves at the base of the plant.

Berry
: A fleshy fruit with one or more seeds, developed from a single ovary.

Biennial
: A plant that lives for two years only, usually producing flowers and seed the second year.

Blade
: The flat, expanded part of the leaf.

Bract
: A modified leaf, often scale-like, usually growing at the base of the flower or on its stalk.

Bristly toothed
: Having a bristle at the tip of each tooth.

Calyx
: The outer whorl of sepals beneath a flower.

Clasping
: Partially surrounding the stem.

Cleft
: Deeply cut, usually past the midpoint.

Compound leaf
: A leaf having two or more leaflets.

Corolla
: The showy part of a flower made up of the individual petals.

Creeper
: A plant growing along the surface of the ground by means of rootlets put out at the nodes.

Disk flowers
: Tiny, tubular flowers growing at the center of a flower head and usually surrounded by ray flowers, as in a Daisy. Collectively they form the disk.

Dissected leaf
: A divided leaf, deeply cut but not reaching the midrib.

Downy
: Having fine, soft hairs.

Entire
: Having a smooth margin, untoothed, not divided.

Family	A group of related plants. Families are divided into genera and genera into species.
Fruit	The mature ovary of a plant, including the seed and other closely associated parts.
Genus	A group of closely related species, a subdivision of a family. The first word in the Latin name of a plant refers to the genus and is always capitalized; the second name gives the species. The plural is "genera."
Glaucous	Having a waxy, whitish bloom or coating.
Head	A dense cluster of little flowers on short stalks or without stalks, such as Clover or the members of the Sunflower Family.
Irregular flower	A flower, such as Clover, having petals or other sets of organs which are not uniform in shape, size, structure, or arrangement.
Joint	The point where the leaf stalk and stem are joined.
Krummholz	The scrub forest just below the treeline.
Lanceolate	Shaped like a lance, narrowing and tapering.
Leaflet	A single division of a compound leaf.
Lip	The upper or lower petal of an irregular flower.
Lobed	Rounded divisions on a leaf or flower, extending less than halfway to the center or base.
Midrib	The central vein of a leaf or leaflet.
Node	The point where the leaf arises from the stem.
Opposite leaves	Leaves arranged in pairs along the stem.
Ovary	The swollen base of the pistil where the seed is produced.
Palate	A raised portion on the lower lip of an irregular flower.
Palmate	Three or more parts radiating from a common center, like fingers on a hand.

Perennial	A plant that renews itself each year by new shoots from the roots or rootstock.
Perfoliate	A leaf that appears to be pierced by its stem.
Petal	An individual segment of a corolla. Petals may be joined at the base or separate.
Petiole	The stalk of a leaf.
Pinnate	Leaflets arranged along both sides of a stem, like feathers.
Pistil	The central female reproductive organ of a flower consisting of the stigma, style and ovary.
Pod	A dry fruit; a capsule.
Pollen	The male sex cells produced by the anther.
Raceme	A cluster of stalked flowers arranged individually along a central stem as in Lily-of-the-valley.
Ray flowers	Petal-like parts encircling the disk in members of the Sunflower Family.
Recurved	Curved backward or downward.
Reflexed	More abruptly recurved.
Rib	One of the principal longitudinal veins of a leaf.
Saprophyte	A plant that derives its food from dead organic material.
Sepal	One unit of a calyx, usually green but may be colored and petal-like.
Sessile	Attached directly at the base, stalkless.
Sheath	A leaf or membrane surrounding a stem.
Spadix	A fleshy spike of tiny flowers.
Spathe	A large bract enclosing a flower cluster.
Species	A distinct kind of plant, a sub-division of a genus.
Spike	An elongated cluster of stalkless flowers.
Spur	A hollow tubular projection from a corolla.
Stamen	The male organ of a flower, made up of a filament and an anther.
Stigma	The tip of the pistil where the pollen is received.
Stipules	Small leaf-like structures at the base of a leaf stalk.
Style	The stalk-like part of the pistil connecting the ovary and the stigma.
Tendril	A thread-like part of a climbing plant, used for support.
Toothed	Having indentations along the margins.

Trailing	Running along the ground but not taking root.
Umbel	A cluster of flowers in which the stalks radiate from the same point like the ribs of an umbrella.
Varieties	Members of a species having minor variations.
Vein	A tiny fluid-carrying channel in a leaf.
Whorled	Three or more leaves or parts arranged in a circle around a central point.

VISUAL GLOSSARY

FLOWER STRUCTURE

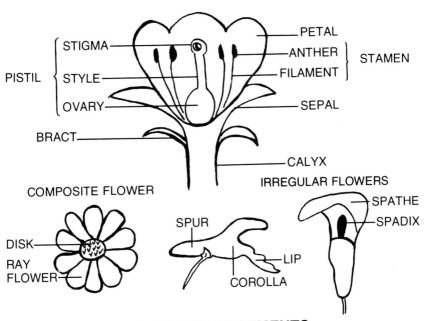

PISTIL { STIGMA, STYLE, OVARY }

PETAL

ANTHER
FILAMENT } **STAMEN**

SEPAL

BRACT

CALYX

COMPOSITE FLOWER

DISK
RAY FLOWER

IRREGULAR FLOWERS

SPATHE
SPADIX

SPUR

LIP
COROLLA

FLOWER ARRANGEMENTS

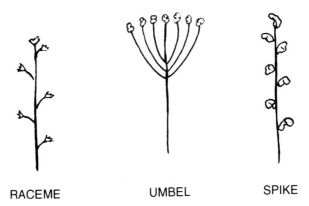

RACEME   UMBEL   SPIKE

LEAF PARTS

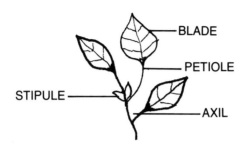

BLADE

PETIOLE

STIPULE

AXIL

LEAF TYPES

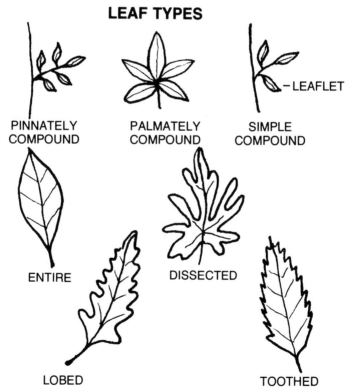

PINNATELY
COMPOUND

PALMATELY
COMPOUND

SIMPLE
COMPOUND

LEAFLET

ENTIRE

DISSECTED

LOBED

TOOTHED

LEAF SHAPES

LINEAR   OVATE   ELLIPTICAL

HEART-SHAPED   ARROW-SHAPED

LANCE-SHAPED   OBLONG

LEAF ARRANGEMENTS

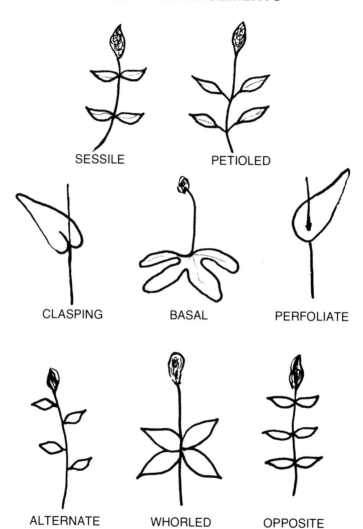

SESSILE

PETIOLED

CLASPING

BASAL

PERFOLIATE

ALTERNATE

WHORLED

OPPOSITE

FLOWER DESCRIPTIONS

Canada Anemone

TRAILING ARBUTUS   WHITE/PINK
Epigaea repens   March–May
Heath Family   Plate 1
Flower: ½″ wide;   **Plant:** creeper

Fragrant white or pink flowers with 5 petals grow in clusters in the leaf axils and at the tips of the hairy stems of this creeping evergreen plant. The oval leaves, ¾–3″ long, are alternate and entire with a leathery appearance and hairy margins.

Trailing Arbutus grows in sandy or rocky woods in acid soil. Also called Mayflower, it is one of the first flowers to bloom in the spring and can often be found flowering beneath the snow. This plant is protected by law and should never be picked. It can be cultivated from seeds collected in early summer.

BLOODROOT   WHITE
Sanguinaria canadensis   April–May
Poppy Family   Plate 1
Flower: 1–1½″ wide;   **Plant:** 6–10″ high

This is a solitary, pure white flower with a golden center, 8–10 petals and a smooth, leafless, orange stem. Growing beside the flower stalk is a single bluish-green leaf, 4–7″ long, with 5–9 lobes. The leaf curls protectively around the bud until it blossoms, after which the leaf unfolds, reaching up to 8″ in width.

Large patches of Bloodroot are often found in rich woods and along stream banks. The flower opens only in bright light and lasts but a short time. The roots and stem have a reddish juice that was once used by Indians as a dye and warpaint.

DUTCHMAN'S BREECHES

Dicentra cucullaria
Poppy Family
Flower: ¾" long; **Plant:** 4–12" high

WHITE
April–May
Plate 1

Suspended from a 5–9" long curving stem are 4–8 waxy, white flowers with yellow tips, drooping in a row and looking like pantaloons hanging upside down from a clothesline. Basal leaves, 3–6" long, feathery, long-stalked, deeply cut and fern-like, are grayish-green on top and paler underneath.

This plant is found in rich woods and on rocky ledges. Squirrel Corn *(D. canadensis),* a similar plant, can often be found nearby but can be recognized by the heart-shaped flower.

SHARP-LOBED HEPATICA

Hepatica acutiloba
Buttercup Family
Flower: ½–1" wide; Plant: 4–6" high

WHITE/PINK/
LAVENDER
April–May
Plate 1

Hepaticas grow singly on hairy stems that arise from a basal rosette of last year's leaves. The flowers have white, pink or lavender petal-like sepals, 3 green, pointed bracts, numerous stamens and several pistils. The olive-green leaves, 2–2½" wide, have 3 pointed lobes.

Look in dry, rocky woods for this plant, which may be half buried in the fallen leaves on the forest floor. The shape of the 3-lobed plant leaf suggests a liver and has given rise to the alternate name, Liverwort. There is a Round-lobed Hepatica *(H. americana)* which lacks the points on the bracts and the leaves.

EARLY SAXIFRAGE   WHITE
Saxifraga virginiensis   April–June
Saxifrage Family   Plate 2
Flower: ¼″ wide;   **Plant:** 4– 16″ high

Early Saxifrage has small clusters of tiny, fragrant white flowers with 5 petals, 5 sepals, 2 pistils and 10 bright yellow stamens, growing at the ends of hairy, branched, leafless stalks. The toothed, egg-shaped leaves, ½–3″ long, are in a basal rosette.

An early spring plant, it can be found growing on dry rocky slopes and outcrops. Its Latin name means "stone breaker" which may refer to where it grows, or to the fact that at one time it was thought to be of value in dissolving kidney stones.

MITERWORT   WHITE
Mitella diphylla   April–June
Saxifrage Family   Plate 2
Flower: ⅙″ wide;   **Plant:** 8– 18″ high

These tiny white flowers with 5 delicately fringed petals are loosely clustered on a long slender stalk. Midway down the stem and opposite one another are 2 stalkless leaves, usually 3-lobed. The basal leaves, also lobed, are up to 3″ in length, oval and long-stalked.

Look for this dainty plant in rich woods. Its name is derived from the miter-shaped fruit capsule which resembles a small cap or bishop's miter. Another common name for it is Bishop's Cap.

DWARF GINSENG
Panax trifolium
Ginseng Family
Flower: $^1/_{12}"$ wide; **Plant:** 4–8" high

WHITE
April–June
Plate 2

This plant has from 15 to 25 tiny, 5-petalled flowers in a small spherical cluster which is dull white at first, but later fades to pink. The stalked leaves are in a whorl of 3, each with 3–5 stalkless leaflets, 1–1½" long, oval and toothed.

Dwarf Ginseng is found in moist woods and clearings. It has yellow berries, and a round root which can be eaten raw or boiled.

WILD STRAWBERRY
Fragaria virginiana
Rose Family
Flower: ¾" wide; **Plant:** creeper

WHITE
April–June
Plate 2

Wild Strawberry has clusters of several small white flowers, each with 5 roundish petals, 5 sepals and many pistils and orange-yellow stamens. The egg-shaped leaves on hairy stems are divided into 3 broad, coarsely toothed, blunt-tipped leaflets, 1–1½" long. Usually the leaf blades are above the flower clusters which grow on leafless 3–6" stems.

This perennial plant is very common in dry pastures and fields, and at the edges of woods. It has seedlike fruits called "achenes" which are deeply imbedded in the edible, round, red, juicy strawberry. Wood Strawberry *(F. vesca),* a similar species, has cone-shaped fruit with seeds on the surface, and sepals that point backward.

HOBBLEBUSH   WHITE
Viburnum alnifolium   April–June
Honeysuckle Family   Plate 3
Flower: to 1″ wide;   **Plant:** 3–10′ high

Flat clusters of small, 5-petalled, showy white flowers grow on the branches of this straggly shrub. The flowers at the edge of the 2–6″ wide cluster are larger than the ones at the center. Large, opposite, heart-shaped leaves, 3–8″ wide, are strongly veined, saw-toothed and have rust-colored hairs on the undersides.

Hobblebush abounds in rich moist woods. Its lower branches curve toward the ground where the tips sometimes take root, creating a snare for the hiker.

MAYAPPLE   WHITE
Podophyllum peltatum   April–June
Barberry Family   Plate 3
Flower: 2″ wide;   **Plant:** 12–18″ high

The single white flower of Mayapple has 6–9 waxy petals and grows from a crotch in the stem beneath 2 very large, deeply cleft, umbrella-like leaves which may reach up to 1′ in width. The plant sometimes produces a nonflowering stalk with only one large leaf.

Very large patches of Mayapple are sometimes found in rich woods and damp shady clearings. Although the leaves, roots and seeds are all very poisonous, the ripe yellow fruit can be used in jellies. Other names by which this plant is known include Mandrake, Wild Lemon and Umbrella Leaf.

TWO-LEAVED TOOTHWORT   WHITE/PINK
Dentaria diphylla   April–June
Mustard Family   Plate 3
Flower: ¾″ wide;   **Plant:** 8–16″ high

These flowers each have 4 white or pink petals and are clustered at the top of an erect stem. Midway on the stalk is a pair of nearly opposite stem leaves, each with 3 broad, toothed segments. The basal leaves are similar and have long stalks.

Toothwort is found in rich moist woods. Other names for it include Crinkleroot and Pepperwort. Its root, which has a peppery taste, has tooth-like projections on it.

WOOD ANEMONE   WHITE/PINK
Anemone quinquefolia   April–June
Buttercup Family   Plate 3
Flower: 1″ wide;   **Plant:** 4–8″ high

The solitary white or pale pink flower of Wood Anemone has 4–9 petal-like sepals and is borne on a slender stem above a whorl of 3 large leaves. The leaves are stalked, sharply toothed and divided into 3–5 segments, each about 1¼″ long.

Large carpets of this small delicate plant can be found in moderately rich soil in open woods. Because of its long slender stem the flower trembles in the smallest breeze; for this reason it is also called Windflower.

LARGE-FLOWERED TRILLIUM
Trillium grandiflorum
Lily Family

WHITE
April–June
Plate 4

Flower: 2–4″ wide; **Plant:** 8–18″ high

Just above a trio of whorled leaves on a short, erect stem, this Trillium bears a large flower, usually white, with 3 large wavy-edged petals, about 2″ long, and 3 smaller green sepals. Variations in petal color, size, shape and number sometimes occur. The leaves are 3–6″ long, broad and pointed. In addition to the prominent lengthwise veins typical of the Lily Family, this and the other Trilliums have cross-veins in their leaves as well.

Also called White Trillium, this flower grows in rich moist woodlands. Its petals turn pink when the flower matures.

PAINTED TRILLIUM
Trillium undulatum
Lily Family

WHITE/PINK
April–June
Plate 4

Flower: 2–2½″ wide; **Plant:** 8–20″ high

Growing on the erect stalk of this plant is a single large flower with 3 white or pinkish wavy-edged petals, 3 green sepals, and 6 stamens with pink tips. Each petal is marked at the base with an inverted crimson V. The leaves are in a whorl of 3 and are stalked, bluish-green, 2½–5″ long, oval and tapered to a sharp point.

Painted Trillium is found in cool, rich, moist woods and swamps. A dark red berry, which ripens in September, has 3 slight angles.

WHITE BANEBERRY
Aetaea pachypoda
Buttercup Family
Flower: ¼" wide;   **Plant:** 1–2' high

WHITE
May–June
Plate 4

The tiny white flowers of this plant are in a dense, oblong cluster, 1–2" long, on top of an erect stem. Each flower has a thick stalk, 4–10 narrow petals and numerous stamens. The leaves are large and divided into many oval, irregularly toothed leaflets.

White Baneberry can be found in rich woods and thickets. It is also called Doll's Eyes because the shiny white berries, which are the fruits, each have a conspicuous black spot causing them to resemble the china eyes of old-fashioned dolls. Red Baneberry *(A. rubra)* is similar but it has a rounder flower cluster with thinner stalks, and bears red berries.

FALSE SOLOMON'S SEAL
Smilacina racemosa
Lily Family
Flower: ⅛" long;   **Plant:** 1–3' high

WHITE
May–June
Plate 4

False Solomon's Seal has many small, fragrant white flowers each with 3 petals, 3 petal-like sepals, and 6 stamens. The flowers are borne in a showy cluster at the end of a gracefully curving stem. The elliptical, pointed leaves are 3–6" long, alternate, parallel-veined and hairy on the undersides.

Look for this plant in damp woods and thickets. The spotted berries which form from the flower clusters turn ruby-red in the fall. The true Solomon's Seals *(Polygonatum* spp.) are very similar but can be recognized by the bell-shaped blossoms which hang singly or in groups along the stem.

WILD SARSAPARILLA

Aralia nudicaulis
Ginseng Family
Flower: ¼″ wide; **Plant:** 8–15″ high

WHITE
May–June
Plate 5

Wild Sarsaparilla usually has 3 round clusters of tiny, greenish-white flowers growing at the tips of a branched, leafless stalk. Occasionally plants will be seen with as many as 7 branches each bearing a flower cluster. A single long-stalked leaf grows beside and above the flowers like an umbrella. This leaf is divided into 3 parts and each part is again divided into 3–5 oval, finely toothed leaflets. Although the flowers and the leaf appear to be on separate stalks, they actually branch off from the plant stem close to the ground.

This plant is common in open woods. The flowers are succeeded by black berries. Its roots are used as a substitute for the true Sarsaparilla *(Smilax officinalis)*.

CANADA MAYFLOWER

Maianthemum canadense
Lily Family
Flower: ⅙″ wide; **Plant:** 3–6″ high

WHITE
May–June
Plate 5

Tiny, white, star-shaped flowers with protruding stamens are in a small dense cluster on the short, often zigzag stem of this plant. The 2–3 broad, light green leaves are 1–3″ long, heart-shaped at the base, and they clasp the stem.

Also called Wild Lily of the Valley, this small woodland plant is common in acid soil of forests and clearings. Plants with only one leaf are immature and will not flower until the second year. The fruit, a green berry, at first is speckled, then bright red. It is cathartic and possibly poisonous.

STARFLOWER

WHITE
May–June
Plate 5

Trientalis borealis
Primrose Family

Flower: ½″ wide;   **Plant:** 4–8″ high

This dainty plant has star-like white flowers on delicate stems which rise above a whorl of 5–9 leaves. Each flower has 7 pointed petals and 7 stamens with golden anthers. The light green leaves are 1¾–4″ long, thin, shiny, lance-shaped and tapered at both ends.

Starflower grows in cool moist woodlands in the spring, but can be found at higher elevations in the summer.

FOAMFLOWER

WHITE
May–June
Plate 5

Tiarella cordifolia
Saxifrage Family

Flower: ¼″ wide;   **Plant:** 6–12″ high

At the top of a leafless stalk this plant bears an elongated, feathery cluster of tiny white flowers, each with 5 narrow petals, 5 sepals and 10 conspicuous stamens. Basal leaves, 2–4″ long, are stalked, sharply toothed, maple-like and usually hairy.

Large colonies of Foamflower can often be found growing in rich woods. Because of its resemblance to Miterwort *(Mitella diphylla)*, this plant is also known as False Miterwort. The genus name *Tiarella* means "little tiara" and refers to the shape of the seed capsule. A tiara was an ancient Persian headdress.

BUNCHBERRY
Cornus canadensis
Dogwood Family
Flower: 1½″ wide;   **Plant:** 3–8″ high

WHITE
May–July
Plate 6

The 4 large, petal-like, white bracts that surround the dense cluster of small greenish-yellow flowers give the impression that this plant has but a single white blossom. Directly beneath the cluster are several tight layers of leaves which appear to be in a whorl. These leaves are actually opposite, and are veined, pointed, oval and 1½–3″ long.

Found in cool moist woods, this plant often forms large colonies. It is also called Ground Dogwood or Dwarf Cornel. Red berries produced by the plant appear in mid-to-late summer.

CANADA ANEMONE
Anemone canadensis
Buttercup Family
Flower: 1–1½″ wide;   **Plant:** 1–1½′ high

WHITE
May–July
Plate 6

This showy, long-stalked flower has 5 broad sepals and a yellow center. The upper and lower stem leaves are stalkless and have 3 deep lobes. The upper leaves are paired, whereas the lower, wedge-shaped ones are in a whorl of 3. The basal leaves are long-stalked and have 5–7 lobes.

Large masses of this Anemone can be found in open wet woods, meadows, thickets and along roadsides. The stalkless stem leaves separate it from other Anemones. The roots of this plant were once used to treat lung diseases and to stop bleeding.

GOLDTHREAD
Coptis groenlandica
Buttercup Family

WHITE
May–July
Plate 6

Flower: ½" wide; **Plant:** 3–6" high

The solitary flower on a long, slender, leafless stem has 5–7 white petal-like sepals, many very small, club-like petals and 15–25 white stamens with golden anthers. Shiny, dark evergreen leaves, 1–2" wide, are divided into 3 scalloped, toothed leaflets.

Goldthread is found in cool woods, bogs and swamps. Its common name refers to the yellow, thread-like underground stem. Another common name, Canker-root, derives from the fact that early settlers and Indians used it to treat mouth sores.

COMMON FLEABANE
Erigeron philadelphicus
Sunflower Family

WHITE/PINK
May–Aug.
Plate 6

Flower: ½–1" wide; **Plant:** 6–36" high

Common Fleabane is an aster-like flower with 100–150 very narrow white or pinkish rays surrounding a flat, yellow central disk. Soft hairs cover the leaves and stems of the plant. The leaves are alternate, oblong to narrowly ovate, and toothed. The basal leaves are up to 6" in length. The upper leaves are smaller and clasp the stem.

This plant is found in rich thickets, fields and open woods. A belief that the dried leaves and plants could repel fleas accounts for the common name. Another name for this flower is Philadelphia Fleabane. The very similar Daisy Fleabane or Sweet Scabious *(E. annuus)* has fewer rays, stiffer stem hairs and upper leaves which do not clasp the stem.

BLADDER CAMPION
Silene cucubalus
Pink Family
Flower: 1″ wide;   **Plant:** 8–18″ high

WHITE
May–Aug.
Plate 7

The many white flowers of this plant are loosely clustered at the ends of the branches. Each flower has 5 petals, which are so deeply cleft that they look like 10, and an inflated, pale green or pink, prominently veined calyx. Protruding from the center of the blossom are 10 long stamens tipped with anthers which turn sepia-brown at maturity. The deep green leaves, 1½–4″ long, are opposite, smooth, ovate to lance-shaped, and often clasp the hairy stem.

Bladder Campion is found in fields, moist meadows and along roadsides. Its common name refers to the shape of the globular calyx.

PARTRIDGEBERRY
Mitchella repens
Bedstraw Family
Flower: ½–⅔″ wide;   **Plant:** creeper

WHITE/PINK
June–July
Plate 7

Pairs of delicate, fragrant, white or pink tubular flowers with 4 spreading lobes are borne at the ends of this plant's creeping stems. The petals have minute hairs on the inside. Small, roundish, shiny evergreen leaves are ½–¾″ long, opposite and white-veined. The plant stems are 4–12″ in length.

Also called Running Box, this attractive plant is found in dry or moist woods. It produces a red, edible, berry-like fruit. A tea made from the leaves was once used by Indian women to induce labor.

WATER ARUM
Calla palustris
Arum Family
Flower: spathe 2″ long; **Plant:** aquatic

WHITE
June–Aug.
Plate 7

What appears to be a large white petal is actually a spathe which partially encloses tiny yellow flowers crowded on a short, club-like spadix. The dark green leaves, up to 6″ long, are glossy, heart-shaped, long-stalked and numerous. The plant stem may protrude 6–12″ above the water.

A very showy aquatic plant, Water Arum can be found in cool bogs, marshes and at the edges of ponds. An attractive cluster of red berries forms after the spathe dries up. The plant is also known as Wild Calla.

TALL MEADOW RUE
Thalictrum polygamum
Buttercup Family
Flower: ⅓″ wide; **Plant:** 2–8′ high

WHITE
June–Aug.
Plate 7

This is a tall plant with loose, branching, plume-like clusters of long-stalked flowers. There are greenish-white sepals which fall early; there are no petals. Numerous erect, thread-like stamens give the blossoms a misty quality. The leaves are bluish to olive-green in color, and are highly divided into roundish, 3-part leaflets, each about 1″ long.

Meadow Rue is common in swamps, in wet meadows and along streams. Although mostly a plant of the lowlands, it can also be found in moist alpine ravines. The female flowers, which are on separate plants, are pollinated by bees and butterflies.

ONE-FLOWERED WINTERGREEN
Moneses uniflora
Wintergreen Family

WHITE
June–Aug.
Plate 8

Flower: ½–¾″ wide; **Plant:** 2–6″ high

One-flowered Wintergreen is a very small plant bearing a single, nodding, fragrant, waxy, white or pink flower. The delicate blossom has 5 slightly pointed petals, 10 white stamens with dull yellow anthers, and a protruding green pistil which bends downward. At the base of the stalk is a rosette of thin, deep green, shiny leaves which are rounded and finely toothed.

Look for this fragile plant in cool moist woods and bogs, where it sometimes grows in large colonies.

SPATULATE-LEAVED SUNDEW
Drosera leucantha
Sundew Family

WHITE
June–Aug.
Plate 8

Flower: ¼″ wide; **Plant:** 4–9″ high

Small, white, 5-petalled flowers grow on one side of the long leafless stalk of this little insectivorous plant. The leaves are in a basal rosette, have red, sticky glandular hairs, and oval blades which are 2–3 times longer than wide. The leaf-stalks are up to 1½″ long and lack hairs.

Sundew is a common plant of acid or peaty bogs. Like Pitcher Plant *(Sarracenia purpurea)*, it is able to survive the poor soil conditions in which it grows by trapping insects and absorbing their juices for nutrients such as nitrogen. A substance exuded by the glandular hairs attracts the insects to the leaves where the tiny, sticky hairs encircle them, preventing their escape. Round-leaved Sundew *(D. rotundifolia)*, which is more common in our area, is very similar but has round leaves and glandular hairs on the leaf-stalks.

ROUND-LEAVED PYROLA
Pyrola rotundifolia
Wintergreen Family

WHITE
June–Aug.
Plate 8

Flowers: ⅔″ wide; **Plant:** 6–15″ high

These fragrant, greenish-white, waxy flowers are in an elongated cluster on an upright stalk. Protruding from each blossom is a long, curving style which bends first downward, then upward. Shiny, olive-green leaves, up to 2¾″ long, are at the base of the plant and are thick, leathery, roundish, evergreen and obscurely toothed. The petioles are often as long as the leaf blades.

Pyrolas are found in dry or moist woods. One-sided Pyrola *(P. secunda)* has flowers growing on one side of the stem. Greenish-flowered Pyrola *(P. virens)* has relatively large, green-veined flowers and small leaves which are usually shorter than their stalks. Shinleaf *(P. elliptica)* is very similar to Round-leaved Pyrola described above but has larger, thinner, duller leaves. The leaf blade is elliptical, rounded at the end and longer than its stalk.

HOARY ALYSSUM
Berteroa incana
Mustard Family

WHITE
June–Sept.
Plate 8

Flower: ¼″ wide; **Plant:** 1–2′ high

Small clusters of tiny white flowers, each with 4 deeply cleft petals, grow in a raceme on this stiffly branched hairy plant. The alternate, lance-shaped leaves, ½–1½″ in length, are stalkless and entire. Both the stem and the leaves are covered with a grayish down.

Look for this common weed in lawns, dry fields, along roadsides and in waste palces. When the flowers fade, oblong, hairy, pointed seedpods develop along the stem. The dried green pods can be used to make attractive winter flower arrangements. After the seeds are released, the empty pods can be picked for decoration.

EVENING LYCHNIS
Lychnis alba
Pink Family
Flower: 1" wide; **Plant:** 1–3' high

WHITE/PINK
June–Sept.
Plate 9

Evening Lychnis has white or pink sweet-scented flowers, each with 5 deeply notched petals. The female flower has an inflated, sticky calyx with 20 very prominent veins and 5 curved protruding styles; the male flower has 10 stamens and a slender calyx with only 10 veins. Male and female flowers are borne on separate plants. The leaves of this highly branching, downy plant are 1½"–4" long, opposite, ovate and hairy.

Also called White Campion, this plant may be found in fields, waste places and along roadsides. It opens at night and is attractive to moths, which serve as pollen carriers between the male and female plants. Night-flowering Catchfly *(Silene noctiflora)* is a very similar flower but it is smaller and has only 3 styles.

FRAGRANT WATER LILY
Nymphaea odorata
Water Lily Family
Flower: 3–5" wide; **Plant:** aquatic

WHITE/PINK
June–Sept.
Plate 9

A very sweet-smelling, floating, showy white or pink blossom, this flower has a bright golden center and numerous tapering petals. Long-stalked leaves, cleft at the base, and 4–12" in diameter, are shiny green on the top and purplish on the underside.

Fragrant Water Lily is very common in the quiet waters of lakes and ponds. Tuberous Water Lily *(N. tuberosa)* is similar, but rarely fragrant. It is 4–8" wide and the leaves are green underneath.

MOUNTAIN SANDWORT
Arenaria groenlandica
Pink Family
Flower: ½" wide; **Plant:** 2–5" high

WHITE
June–Sept.
Plate 9

Small, white translucent flowers, each with 5 slightly notched petals, grow on slender stalks arising from this low plant. The leaves are ½" in length, opposite and very narrow. At the base of the stem the leaves grow in tufts.

A very conspicuous mat-forming plant of higher mountains, this Sandwort is common in rock crevices and gravelly sites, particularly above the treeline. This species is considered an alpine plant and has special adaptations for growing in a harsh environment. It is protected from the drying effects of the cold winds of the mountain by growing close to the ground and in protected niches in the rocks. It has no adaptation, however, to prevent its destruction from trampling. Hikers are urged to walk carefully.

YARROW
Achillea millefolium
Sunflower Family
Flower: ¼" wide; **Plant:** 1–3' high

WHITE/PINK
June–Sept.
Plate 9

The small white flowers of this plant have 4–6 rays and grow in tight, flat-topped clusters on a woolly plant. Occasionally pink forms are seen. The gray-green leaves are lance-shaped, soft, fern-like and very finely dissected. The stem leaves are up to 6" long and the basal ones are longer.

Yarrow, also called Milfoil, can be found along roadsides and in old fields. It was once used to treat fever, bleeding, rashes and stomach disorders. The crushed leaves are aromatic, and they were used for snuff at one time. The dried flower heads make attractive additions to winter bouquets. Picked early, the pods will have a golden brown hue, later they will be a deeper brown.

QUEEN ANNE'S LACE
Daucus carota
Parsley Family
Flower: ⅛" wide; **Plant:** 1–3′ high

WHITE
June–Sept.
Plate 10

These tiny, creamy-white flowers are in an extremely flat, lace-like cluster, 3–5" wide. At or near the center of the cluster there is usually one purplish floret and beneath the cluster there are stiff, 3-forked, leaf-like bracts. The leaves, 2–8" long, are highly divided, feathery and fern-like. The stem is covered with bristly hairs.

One of our most common weeds, this attractive biennial grows in dry fields and waste places. The garden carrot was derived from this plant, which is often called Wild Carrot. Its first year taproot is edible when cooked. The old flower heads curl inward looking somewhat like the nests of birds, hence another common name is Bird's Nest.

INDIAN PIPE
Monotropa uniflora
Indian Pipe Family
Flower: ½–1" long; **Plant:** 3–9" high

WHITE
June–Sept.
Plate 10

Nodding from the top of the thick, translucent, bract-covered stem of this plant is a single flower with 4–5 white or salmon-pink petals, 10–12 stamens and a single pistil.

This non-green, waxy, saprophytic plant is found growing in woodland humus where it derives nourishment from decaying organic matter. It turns black when the fruit ripens, or when picked and dried. An early Indian herb doctor is said to have used the juice of the plant stem mixed with water to treat problems of the eyes.

PIPSISSEWA
WHITE/PINK

Chimaphila umbellata
July–Aug.

Wintergreen Family
Plate 10

Flower: ½″ wide; **Plant:** 4–10″ high

In a small loose cluster at the top of the stem, this plant has several fragrant, waxy, white or pinkish flowers with reddish anthers, and 5 cup-shaped, spreading petals with rounded tips. Several whorls of shiny, dark evergreen, finely toothed leaves are on a single stem. The leaves are wider toward the tips and vary in length from 1–2½″.

Also called Prince's Pine, this is a small erect plant found in both dry and moist woods, where it often grows in large patches.

WINTERGREEN
WHITE

Gaultheria procumbens
July–Aug.

Heath Family
Plate 10

Flower: ⅓″ long; **Plant:** creeper

This low plant has upright branches from which one or more small, waxy, white, 5-lobed, bell-shaped flowers hang, partially hidden beneath the thick, shiny, oval, slightly toothed leaves, 1–2″ long.

Small colonies of this evergreen shrub are formed in woods and clearings by creeping underground stems. The plant produces a bright red, edible fruit which may persist all winter. An extract from Wintergreen (also called Checkerberry and Teaberry) is used to flavor teas, candy and gum.

COMMON ARROWHEAD
Sagittaria latifolia
Water Plantain Family
Flower: 2–3″ wide; **Plant:** aquatic, 1–4′ high

WHITE
July–Sept.
Plate 11

The flowers of this aquatic plant grow in whorls of 3 on a tall stalk, have 3 petals, 3 sepals and a golden yellow center. Growing from the base of the stalk are bright green, arrow-shaped leaves, 2–16″ long. The leaves may vary from broad to lance-shaped to linear, and may have 2 long backward-projecting lobes, or may lack lobes entirely.

Arrowhead is found along the edges of ponds, bogs and small streams. Because ducks feed on the starchy, potato-like tubers of the underground stem, it is also called Duck Potatoes.

CANADIAN BURNET
Sanguisorba canadensis
Rose Family
Flower: ¼″ wide; **Plant:** 1–5′ high

WHITE
July–Sept.
Plate 11

Borne in slender, dense, feathery spikes, 1–6″ in length, these flowers have 4 petal-like sepals, 4 long protruding stamens and one pistil. The pinnately compound, toothed, stalked, oval leaves, 1–3″ long, have 7–15 leaflets.

This plant grows only in wet places such as bogs, swamps and low meadows. The plant juice was once believed to be of value in stopping bleeding. *Sanguisorba*, the Latin generic name for the Burnets, means "to drink up blood."

VIRGIN'S BOWER
Clematis virginiana
Buttercup Family

WHITE
July–Sept.
Plate 11

Flower: 1″ wide;   **Plant:** vine

Clusters of white flowers with 4–5 petal-like sepals and many conspicuous stamens grow from the leaf axils of this climbing vine. Dark green, veined leaves are divided into 3 coarsely toothed leaflets, each about 2″ long. The plant supports itself by leaf-stalks that wind around other plants.

Virgin's Bower grows at the edges of woods, in thickets and along stream banks. In the fall, gray, silky plumes adhere to the seeds, looking somewhat like beards, hence the other name for this plant, Old Man's Beard. Susceptible persons may get an allergic reaction to the leaves of the plant.

TURTLEHEAD
Chelone glabra
Snapdragon Family

WHITE
July–Sept.
Plate 11

Flower: 1–1½″ long;   **Plant:** 1–3′ high

At the top of a smooth stem, this plant bears a tight cluster of swollen, white flowers, tinged with crimson or pink at the tips. Each individual flower, with the upper lip arching over the hairy lower one, resembles a turtle's head. The lance-shaped leaves, 3–6″ long, are paired, short-stalked and sharp-toothed.

Look for this plant in wet places, such as along stream banks or near roadside ditches.

BOUNCING BET   WHITE/PINK
Saponaria officinalis   July–Sept.
Pink Family   Plate 12
Flower: 1″ wide;   **Plant:** 1–2½′ high

Bouncing Bet has clusters of fragrant white or pale pink flowers at the top of a smooth, stout stem which is swollen at the joints. Each flower has 5 or more reflexed petals, indented at the tips, and a 5-lobed calyx. Sometimes the number of petals is doubled. The smooth oval leaves, 2–3″ long, are opposite, and each has 3–5 prominent veins. The plant is slightly branched.

Large colonies of this perennial are often found along roadsides and in waste places. It is also called Soapwort because a soap can be made from its leaves. The common name Bouncing Bet comes from an old-fashioned term for a washerwoman.

BONESET   WHITE
Eupatorium perfoliatum   July–Sept.
Sunflower Family   Plate 12
Flower: heads ¼″ long;   **Plant:** 2–4′ high

At the top of a hairy stem this tall, erect plant has a dense, flat-topped cluster of many dull white flowers. The leaves, 4–8″ long, are lanced-shaped, wrinkled, toothed, opposite and joined at the base, making it appear that they are pierced by the stem.

Boneset, also known as Thoroughwort, is found in thickets and wet meadows. Herb doctors once believed that plants with united leaves could heal broken bones, hence the common name Boneset.

PEARLY EVERLASTING
Anaphalis margaritacea
Sunflower Family

WHITE
July–Sept.
Plate 12

Flower: heads ¼–½″ wide;   **Plant:** 1–3′ high

The small, white globular heads of Pearly Everlasting grow in a crowded cluster at the tip of a white-woolly upright stem. Each head is made up of all disk flowers, and has a central yellow tuft and petal-like bracts. Narrow, sage green leaves, 3–5″ long, are alternate, and white-woolly on the undersides.

Look for this plant in dry pastures, waste places, on banks and along roadsides. It is especially attractive when used in dried arrangements. If picked early and dried, the flowers will stay pure white throughout the winter.

FLAT-TOPPED WHITE ASTER
Aster umbellatus
Sunflower Family

WHITE
Aug.–Sept.
Plate 12

Flower: heads ½–¾″ wide;   **Plant:** 1–7′ high

Numerous flower heads grow in a wide, flat-topped cluster, up to 1′ across, on the rigid, erect stem of this plant. Each flower has 10–15 backward-curving white ray flowers surrounding a central yellow disk, which turns purplish with age. The toothless leaves, up to 6″ in length, are elliptical or lance-shaped, tapered at both ends, and have rough margins.

This is the earliest Aster to bloom and can be found in late summer in wet meadows, at the edges of swamps and in moist shady places.

CAROLINA SPRING BEAUTY

PINK/WHITE
April–May
Plate 13

Claytonia caroliniana
Purslane Family

Flower: ½–¾" wide; **Plant:** 6–12" high

These fragile pink or white flowers have 5 petals striped with dark pink, 5 stamens with pink anthers, and are borne in loose clusters at the ends of the stalks. The dark green, short-stemmed, oblong to oval leaves, 2–8" long, are usually paired.

In early spring in moist open woods one can find this attractive perennial growing in large masses. In the higher mountains it may be found blooming as late as mid-August. Deer browse on the leaves and flowers of the plant, and rodents eat the bulbs. A similar species, Spring Beauty *(C. virginica)* has grass-like leaves and is usually pink.

ROSE TWISTED-STALK

PINK
April–July
Plate 13

Streptopus roseus
Lily Family

Flower: ⅓" long; **Plant:** 1–3' high

Nodding, rose-pink, 6-pointed and bell-like, these flowers are on short stems which are bent or "twisted" near the middle. The flowers hang singly from a point near each leaf axil. The broad, lance-shaped leaves, 2½–6" long, are sessile, parallel-veined and arranged alternately on a forked, zig-zag, arching stem.

An easily recognized plant, it can be found in cool moist woods and thickets. Rosybells and Pink or Rose Mandarin are other names for this flower.

PINK LADY'S SLIPPER

Cypripedium acaule
Orchid Family

PINK
May–June
Plate 13

Flower: 2½" long; **Plant:** 6–15" high

Borne singly on a leafless stalk, this pink, slipper-like flower has an inflated petal which is veined with red and indented down the middle. The sepals and side petals are greenish-brown and spreading. Arising from the base of the plant are 2 large, oval leaves, up to 8" long.

Look for this Orchid in acid woods, oak and pine forests, and bogs. It is sometimes called Mocassin Flower and also Stemless Orchid, the latter due to the fact that the leaves arise from the root and not from the plant stem.

GAYWINGS

Polygala paucifolia
Milkwort Family

PINK
May–June
Plate 13

Flower: ¾" long; **Plant:** 3–7" high

Small, dainty pink flowers are clustered in the axils of the upper leaves of this plant. Each flower has 3 petals united in a hollow tube with a yellow, bushy fringe at the tip of the lowest petal. Flaring "wings" are formed by 2 lateral sepals. Broad evergreen leaves, ¾–1½" long, oval, alternate and untoothed are crowded at the top of the stem. The lower leaves are reduced and bract-like.

Also known as Fringed Polygala and Flowering Wintergreen, this low plant grows in rich moist woods.

HEDGE BINDWEED

PINK/WHITE

Convolvulus sepium

May–Sept.

Morning Glory Family

Plate 14

Flower: 2–3″ wide;   **Plant:** vine

The flowers of Hedge Bindweed are pink or white, or pale pink with white stripes. They are borne singly on a long stalk, have 5 fused petals, and are funnel-shaped. Grayish-green leaves, 2–4″ long, are triangular with blunt basal lobes.

This smooth, twining vine is common on roadsides and in fields and thickets where it is generally considered a nuisance because of its tendency to climb over all other plants. Its showy blossom resembles the garden Morning Glory *(Ipomoea purpurea)*.

TWINFLOWER

PINK

Linnaea borealis

June–July

Honeysuckle Family

Plate 14

Flower: ½″ long;   **Plant:** creeper

Twinflower has a pair of nodding, bell-like, fragrant, pink flowers growing at the top of each short, erect, hairy stalk. The stalks are very slender, 3–6″ long, and arise from a slightly woody stem. Leaves are roundish, light green, opposite, toothed, and they are under 1″ in length.

This is a low evergreen vine which grows in cool woods and bogs at lower elevations, and it often extends into the scrub forest or krummholtz, that area of dwarf trees just below the tree line in the mountains. A favorite flower of Carolus Linnaeus (1707–1778), the father of modern botany, it was named in honor of him.

COMMON WOOD SORREL
Oxalis montana
Wood Sorrel Family

PINK/WHITE
June–July
Plate 14

Flower: ¾" wide;   **Plant:** 3–6" high

Borne singly on delicate stems, 3–6" long, are these pink or white flowers, which are strongly veined with deep pink and have 5 petals, each with an indentation at the tip. The basal, clover-like leaves have 3 heart-shaped leaflets, each about ½" wide.

Wood Sorrel is an attractive flower of rich damp woods. It often grows in very large patches. The leaves, which close at night, have a sour taste.

SHEEP LAUREL
Kalmia angustifolia
Heath Family

PINK
June–July
Plate 14

Flower: ⅓–½" wide;   **Plant:** 1–3' high

A low evergreen shrub, this plant bears a dense cluster of small, saucer-shaped flowers, each with 5 deep pink petals and 10 stamens. Below the newer, upright leaves the flower cluster encircles the stem. The leaves below the cluster are darker and drooping. The dull, olive-green leaves, 1½–2" long, are elliptical or oblong, grow in whorls of 3 and are lighter beneath when mature.

Large stands of this shrub are often found in old fields and bogs. Because the foliage is poisonous to livestock, the plant is also called Lambkill. The flowers of Mountain Laurel *(K. latifolia)* and Swamp Laurel *(K. polifolia)* are very similar and have in common an interesting mechanism for pollen distribution. The anthers of the 10 stamens are contained in 10 small pouches of the corolla. When touched by an insect these anthers pop out releasing pollen over the visitor who may then carry it to the stigma of another flower.

COMMON MILKWEED PINK/PURPLE
Asclepias syriaca June–Aug.
Milkweed Family Plate 15
Flower: ½" wide; **Plant:** 2–6' high

These sweet-scented flowers grow in various soft shades of pink or purple and are borne in rounded, sometimes drooping, clusters in the upper leaf axils and at the top of the plant. Light green, opposite leaves, 4–10" long, are thick, broad and oval with gray down on the undersides. The plant stem and leaves exude a milky juice when broken.

Milkweed is common in old fields, waste places and along roadsides. It is the chief source of food for the larvae of the Monarch butterfly.

PASTURE ROSE PINK
Rosa carolina June–Aug.
Rose Family Plate 15
Flower: 2–3" wide; **Plant:** 1–3' high

A showy, slender-stemmed Rose, this plant has fragrant, solitary pink flowers with 5 petals which are broad at the tips and slightly indented. The smooth leaves are divided into 3–7 oval, dull green, coarsely toothed leaflets, At the base of each leaf stalk there are narrow stipules. Straight, slender thorns, which grow only at the points where the leaves branch off from the stem, are an identifying feature.

Pasture Rose is a very common low, branching wild Rose found in open woods and dry pastures.

ROSE POGONIA   PINK
Pogonia ophioglossoides   June–Aug.
Orchid Family   Plate 15
Flower: 1¾″ long; **Plant:** 3–24″ high

This solitary, rose-pink Orchid, at the end of a slender greenish stem, has petals and sepals of equal size. The petals have a silky texture and a delicate fragrance. A distinctive feature is the lower lip which is deeply fringed, and bearded in the center with yellow bristles. Clasping the middle of the stalk is a single oblong leaf up to 4¾″ in length. A leaf-like bract grows below the flower.

Also known as Snakemouth, Rose Pogonia is found in sphagnum bogs, wet meadows, swamps and along shores. It is one of the more common Orchids.

DEPTFORD PINK   PINK
Dianthus armeria   June–Aug.
Pink Family   Plate 15
Flower: ½″ wide; **Plant:** 6–24″ high

A slender plant, Deptford Pink has, at the top of a stiff erect stem, flat-topped clusters of deep pink flowers, each with 5 white-dotted, ragged-edged petals. Needle-like, light green leaves, 1–4″ long, are very narrow and erect.

This is a plant of dry fields and roadsides. Maiden Pink *(D. deltoides)*, a related species, has larger, solitary flowers. Its common name refers to Deptford, England where it once grew in abundance.

2

PHOTO
SECTION

Bloodroot

1. Trailing Arbutus March–May
Epigaea repens Page 2

2. Bloodroot April–May
Sanguinaria canadensis Page 2

3. Dutchman's Breeches April–May
Dicentra cucullaria Page 3

4. Sharp-lobed Hepatica April–May
Hepatica acutiloba Page 3

PLATE 2

35

1. Early Saxifrage   April–June
   Saxifraga virginiensis   Page 4

2. Miterwort   April–June
   Mitella diphylla   Page 4

3. Dwarf Ginseng   April–June
   Panax trifolium   Page 5

4. Wild Strawberry   April–June
   Fragaria virginiana   Page 5

1. Hobblebush   April–June
Viburnum alnifolium   Page 6

2. Mayapple   April–June
Podophyllum peltatum   Page 6

3. Two-leaved Toothwort   April–June
Dentaria diphylla   Page 7

4. Wood Anemone   April–June
Anemone quinquefolia   Page 7

PLATE 4

1. Large-flowered Trillium   April–June
   Trillium grandiflorum   Page 8

2. Painted Trillium   April–June
   Trillium undulatum   Page 8

3. White Baneberry 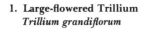   May–June
   Actaea pachypoda   Page 9

4. False Solomon's Seal   May–June
   Smilacina racemosa   Page 9

1. Wild Sarsaparilla   May–June
   Aralia nudicaulis   Page 10

2. Canada Mayflower   May–June
   Maianthemum canadense   Page 10

3. Starflower   May–June
   Trientalis borealis   Page 11

4. Foamflower   May–June
   Tiarella cordifolia   Page 11

PLATE 6

39

| 1. **Bunchberry** | May–July | 2. **Canada Anemone** | May–July |
| *Cornus canadensis* | Page 12 | *Anemone canadensis* | Page 12 |

| 3. **Goldthread** | May–July | 4. **Common Fleabane** | May–Aug. |
| *Coptis groenlandica* | Page 13 | *Erigeron philadelphicus* | Page 13 |

1. Bladder Campion  May–Aug.
   Silene cucubalus Page 14

2. Partridgeberry June–July
   Mitchella repens Page 14

3. Water Arum June–Aug.
   Calla palustris Page 15

4. Tall Meadow Rue   June–Aug.
   Thalictrum polygamum Page 15

PLATE 8

41

1. **One-flowered Wintergreen** June–Aug.
   Moneses uniflora Page 16

2. **Spatulate-leaved Sundew** June–Aug.
   Drosera leucantha Page 16

3. **Round-leaved Pyrola** √ June–Aug.
   Pyrola rotundifolia Page 17

4. **Hoary Alyssum**√ June–Sept.
   Berteroa incana Page 17

1. **Evening Lychnis**   June–Sept.
   Lychnis alba   Page 18

2. **Fragrant Water Lily**   June–Sept.
   Nymphaea odorata   Page 18

3. **Mountain Sandwort**   June–Sept.
   Arenaria groenlandica   Page 19

4. **Yarrow**   June–Sept.
   Achillea millefolium   Page 19

PLATE 10

43

1. **Queen Anne's Lace** √   June–Sept.
   Daucus carota   Page 20

2. **Indian Pipe** √   June–Sept.
   Monotropa uniflora   Page 20

3. **Pipsissewa**   July–Aug.
   Chimaphila umbellata Page 21

4. **Wintergreen** √   July–Aug.
   Gaultheria procumbens Page 21

1. **Common Arrowhead**   July–Sept.
   Sagittaria latifolia   Page 22

2. **Canadian Burnet**   July–Sept.
   Sanguisorba canadensis   Page 22

3. **Virgin's Bower**   July–Sept.
   Clematis virginiana   Page 23

4. **Turtlehead**   July–Sept.
   Chelone glabra   Page 23

PLATE 12

45

1. Bouncing Bet   July–Sept.
Saponaria officinalis   Page 24

2. Boneset   July–Sept.
Eupatorium perfoliatum   Page 24

3. Pearly Everlasting   July–Sept.
Anaphalis margaritacea   Page 25

4. Flat-topped White Aster   Aug–Sept.
Aster umbellatus   Page 25

1. Carolina Spring Beauty April–May
Claytonia caroliniana Page 26

2. Rose Twisted-stalk April–July
Streptopus roseus Page 26

3. Pink Lady's Slipper May–June
Cypripedium acaule Page 27

4. Gaywings May–June
Polygala paucifolia Page 27

PLATE 14   47

1. **Hedge Bindweed**   May–Sept.
   Convolvulus sepium   Page 28

2. **Twinflower**   June–July
   Linnaea borealis   Page 28

3. **Common Wood Sorrel**   June–July
   Oxalis montana   Page 29

4. **Sheep Laurel**   June–July
   Kalmia angustifolia   Page 29

1. Common Milkweed June–Aug.
Asclepias syriaca Page 30

2. Pasture Rose June–Aug.
Rosa carolina Page 30

3. Rose Pogonia June–Aug.
Pogonia ophioglossoides Page 31

4. Deptford Pink June–Aug.
Dianthus armeria Page 31

PLATE 16   49

1. **Meadowsweet**   June–Sept.
   Spiraea latifolia   Page 66

2. **Fireweed**   July–Sept.
   Epilobium angustifolium   Page 66

3. **Water Smartweed**   July–Sept.
   Polygonum amphibium   Page 67

4. **Spotted Joe-Pye Weed** ⱽ   July–Sept.
   Eupatorium maculatum   Page 67

1. **Steeplebush**   July–Sept.
   Spiraea tomentosa   Page 68

2. **Heal-all**   May–Sept.
   Prunella vulgaris   Page 68

3. **Purple-flowering Raspberry** Jun.–Aug.
   Rubus odoratus   Page 69

4. **Spotted Knapweed** ✓   June–Aug.
   Centaurea maculosa   Page 69

PLATE 18

51

1. Swamp Milkweed
Asclepias incarnata

June–Aug.
Page 70

2. Purple Loosestrife √
Lythrum salicaria

June–Sept.
Page 70

3. Purple Fringed Orchid
Habenaria fimbriata

July–Aug.
Page 71

4. Wild Ginger
Asarum canadense

April–June
Page 71

PLATE 19

1. **Red Trillium**
   Trillium erectum
   April–June
   Page 72

2. **Wild Columbine**
   Aquilegia canadensis
   April–July
   Page 72

3. **Northern Pitcher Plant**
   Sarracenia purpurea
   June–July
   Page 73

4. **Cardinal Flower**
   Lobelia cardinalis
   July–Sept.
   Page 73

PLATE 20

53

1. Blue Cohosh   April–June
   Caulophyllum thalictroides   Page 74

2. Jack-in-the-pulpit   April–June
   Arisaema atrorubens   Page 74

3. Hairy Solomon's Seal   May–June
   Polygonatum pubescens   Page 75

4. Indian Cucumber Root   May–July
   Medeola virginiana   Page 75

1. Coltsfoot   March–June
Tussilago farfara   Page 76

2. Marsh Marigold   April–June
Caltha palustris   Page 76

3. Wild Oats   April–June
Uvularia sessilifolia   Page 77

4. Barren Strawberry   April–June
Waldsteinia fragarioides   Page 77

PLATE 22

55

1. **Golden Alexanders**
   Zizia aurea
   April–June
   Page 78

2. **Trout Lily**
   Erythronium americanum
   April–June
   Page 78

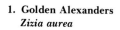

3. **Clintonia**
   Clintonia borealis
   May–July
   Page 79

4. **Rough-fruited Cinquefoil**
   Potentilla recta
   May–Aug.
   Page 79

1. **Yellow Goatsbeard**   May–Aug.
   Tragopogon pratensis   Page 80

2. **Yellow Pond Lily**   May–Sept.
   Nuphar variegatum   Page 80

3. **Swamp Candles**   June–Aug.
   Lysimachia terrestris   Page 81

4. **Sundrops**   June–Aug.
   Oenothera fruticosa   Page 81

PLATE 24   57

1. Fringed Loosestrife   June–Aug.
   Lysimachia ciliata   Page 82

2. Birdsfoot Trefoil   June–Sept.
   Lotus corniculatus   Page 82

3. Common St. Johnswort   June–Sept.
   Hypericum perforatum   Page 83

4. Common Mullein   June–Sept.
   Verbascom thapsus   Page 83

1. **Evening Primrose** June–Sept.
   Oenothera biennis Page 84

2. **Butter-and-eggs** June–Oct.
   Linaria vulgaris Page 84

3. **Black-eyed Susan** June–Oct.
   Rudbeckia hirta Page 85

4. **Green-headed Coneflower** July–Sept.
   Rudbeckia laciniata Page 85

PLATE 26

59

1. Goldenrod July–Oct.
Solidago Page 86

2. Orange Hawkweed June–Sept.
Hieracium aurantiacum Page 86

3. Butterfly Weed July–Aug.
Asclepias tuberosa Page 87

4. Spotted Touch-me-not July–Sept.
Impatiens capensis Page 87

1. Marsh Blue Violet   April–June
Viola cucullata   Page 88

2. Bluets   April–July
Houstonia caerulea   Page 88

3. Blue Flag   May–July
Iris versicolor   Page 89

4. Cow Vetch   May–Aug.
Vicia cracca   Page 89

PLATE 28   61

1. Common Speedwell   May–Aug.
   Veronica officinalis   Page 90

2. Common Blue-eyed Grass   June–July
   Sisyrinchium montanum   Page 90

3. Harebell   June–Sept.
   Campanula rotundifolia   Page 91

4. Viper's Bugloss   June–Sept.
   Echium vulgare   Page 91

1. Chicory   June–Oct.
Cichorium intybus   Page 92

2. Pickerelweed   June–Oct.
Pontederia cordata   Page 92

3. Creeping Bellflower   July–Sept.
Campanula rapunculoides   Page 93

4. Blue Vervain   July–Sept.
Verbena hastata   Page 93

PLATE 30

63

1. New York Aster   July–Oct.
  Aster novi-belgii   Page 94

2. Blue Curls   Aug.–Oct.
  Trichostema dichotomum   Page 94

3. Blind Gentian   Aug.–Oct.
  Gentiana clausa   Page 95

4. Fringed Gentian   Sept.–Oct.
  Gentiana crinita   Page 95

3

FLOWER DESCRIPTIONS

Wild Oats

MEADOWSWEET
PINK/WHITE

Spiraea latifolia
June–Sept.

Rose Family
Plate 16

Flower: ¼″ wide; **Plant:** 2–5′ high

The pale pink or white flowers of this woody shrub have 5 petals, 5 sepals and numerous prominent, pink-red stamens. They grow in a dense, branching cluster at the top of a sturdy stem. The light green, sharply toothed leaves are 1½–2¾″ long, nearly smooth, alternate, ovate, and pale on the undersides.

Meadowsweet can be found in old fields, meadows and along roadsides, usually in low moist ground. Steeplebush *(S. tomentosa),* a similar shrub, has a narrower and tighter rose-pink flower cluster, and the stems and undersides of the leaves are very woolly. Narrowleaf Meadowsweet *(S. alba)* has narrower leaves and white flowers.

FIREWEED
PINK

Epilobium angustifolium
July–Sept.

Evening Primrose Family
Plate 16

Flower: 1″ wide; **Plant:** 3–7′ high

Growing in a terminal, spike-like cluster at the top of a long stem, this plant has deep pink flowers, each with 4 roundish, spreading petals. Narrow, alternate, willow-like leaves, up to 8″ long, are green on top and pale gray below.

Fireweed is found in cleared woodlands, fields, waste places and along roadsides. It is especially common on land that has recently been burned over. The flowers, which open slowly up the stem over more than a month, are replaced as they fade by long, reddish seedpods which angle upward. The new shoots and leaves can be used as a substitute for asparagus. The plant is also called Great Willow Herb.

WATER SMARTWEED
Polygonum amphibium
Buckwheat Family
Flower: ¹/₆″ long; **Plant:** aquatic

PINK
July–Sept.
Plate 16

These tiny, deep pink flowers lack petals, have a 5-part calyx and are tightly packed in a stubby, spike-like cluster about 1″ long and ½″ wide. The floating oval leaves are short-pointed or blunt, rounded at their bases and up to 6″ long. At each leaf joint on the stem there is a swelling and an encircling sheath.

Look for this aquatic species in ponds and quiet streams. Swamp Smartweed *(P. coccineum)* is similar but has a longer (1½–6″) flower spike. Both of these Smartweeds have terrestrial forms.

SPOTTED JOE-PYE WEED
Eupatorium maculatum
Sunflower Family
Flower: heads ⅓″ wide; **Plant:** 2–6′ high

PINK/PURPLE
July–Sept.
Plate 16

The fuzzy flower heads of this plant are in a large flat-topped cluster which ranges in color from dusty pink to pale purple. The sturdy stem is deep purple or purple spotted and is not glaucous. Leaves, 2½–8″ long, usually in whorls of 3–5, are thick, lance-shaped and coarsely toothed.

This Joe-Pye Weed is commonly found in wet thickets and meadows. There are several similar species in our area. Sweet Joe-Pye Weed *(E. purpureum)* usually has a green stem which is purplish or black only at the leaf joints. When crushed, the foliage smells like vanilla. Hollow Joe-Pye Weed *(E. fistulosom)* has a smooth hollow stem tinged with purple and covered with a whitish bloom. The plant is thought to be named for an Indian, "Joe Pye," who used it for curing fevers.

STEEPLEBUSH   PINK
Spiraea tomentosa   July–Sept.
Rose Family   Plate 17
Flower: ¹/₆″ wide;   **Plant:** 2–4′ high

Steeplebush has a long, slender, fuzzy spike of densely packed, branched clusters of deep pink flowers, each with 5 petals, 5 sepals and numerous stamens. The flowers bloom from the top of the spike down. Egg-shaped, toothed leaves, 1–2″ long, are olive-green on top and brownish and very woolly underneath. The woody, reddish stem is also woolly.

A tall erect shrub, this plant is found in old fields, pastures and on low ground. Sometimes it is confused with Meadowsweet *(S. latifolia)* but it can be recognized by the woolly undersides of its leaves and the spike, which is narrower and more tightly packed. Another name for this plant is Hardhack.

HEAL-ALL   PURPLE
Prunella vulgaris   May–Sept.
Mint Family   Plate 17
Flower: ½″ long;   **Plant:** 6–12″ high

The tiny, purple, hooded flowers of this plant have an arched upper lip and a slightly fringed lower lip. The blossoms are borne in an erect, dense, oblong, square-stemmed spike, which elongates after flowering takes place. Opposite leaves, 1–3″ long, are ovate and slightly toothed or toothless.

Heal-all is a low, sometimes sprawling, plant of fields, lawns and roadsides. It is thought to cure throat ailments. Another name for it is Selfheal.

PURPLE-FLOWERING RASPBERRY   PURPLE/PINK
Rubus odoratus   June–Aug.
Rose Family   Plate 17
Flower: 1–2″ wide;   **Plant:** 3–6′ high

This thornless shrub has loose clusters of pinkish-purple flowers, each with 5 broad, rose-like petals and numerous stamens and pistils. As the flowers mature they become more purple. Large, maple-shaped leaves have 3–5 lobes and are from 4–10″ wide. The stems are reddish-brown and have sticky hairs.

Purple-flowering Raspberry is a common plant which can be found growing in dry woods and thickets. The large maple-like leaves distinguish it from the various wild Roses which the flower resembles. The flat, red berries of the plant are dry and acid.

SPOTTED KNAPWEED   PURPLE/PINK
Centaurea maculosa   June–Aug.
Sunflower Family   Plate 17
Flower: heads 1″ wide   **Plant:** 2–3′ high

A highly branched plant, Spotted Knapweed has purple or pink (sometimes white) thistle-like flower heads with pale, prickly, black-tipped bracts. The stem is wiry and covered with soft hairs. The leaves are deeply cleft; the lower ones 4–8″ long, the upper ones smaller.

Introduced from Europe, this flower is now widespread throughout our area. It can be found in fields, waste places and along roadsides. Cornflower *(C. cyanus),* also called Blue Bottle or Bachelor's Buttons, is a similar annual. It has solitary flowers on long, loose branches. The margins of the outer bracts are toothed and whitish. The flowers vary in color but are most often blue.

SWAMP MILKWEED   PURPLE
Asclepias incarnata   June–Aug.
Milkweed Family   Plate 18
Flower: ¼" wide;   **Plant:** 1–4′ high

At the end of a tall branching stem, this plant has a flat-topped cluster of purplish flowers with 5 reflexed petals and a whitish, 5-part, elevated crown. The many leaves are narrow, lance-shaped, short-stalked and up to 4" long. The leaf veins form an acute angle with the midrib.

This plant is very common in swamps and other wet areas. Its juice is less milky than that of the other Milkweeds.

PURPLE LOOSESTRIFE   PURPLE/PINK
Lythrum salicaria   June–Sept.
Loosestrife Family   Plate 18
Flower: ½–¾" wide;   **Plant:** 2–4′ high

Growing in a tall, dense, tapering spike on an erect stem, these pinkish-purple flowers each have 4–6 wrinkled petals. Usually there will be the same number of stamens as there are petals; however, the number will sometimes be double. The leaves are opposite or whorled, unstalked, lanceolate and 1½–4" long. The lower ones are downy and clasp the stem slightly.

A showy perennial, this Loosestrife often covers large areas in wet meadows and roadside ditches, successfully crowding out other summer flowers. The dried pods can be used in bouquets for interesting color, texture and height.

LARGE PURPLE FRINGED ORCHID

Habenaria fimbriata
Orchid Family

PURPLE
July–Aug.
Plate 18

Flower: 1″ long; **Plant:** 2–4′ high

Borne in a spike, 2–2½″ in diameter, at the top of a leafy stem, are many rose-purple flowers, each with a 3-lobed, deeply fringed lip petal, 2 lateral petals and a backward-pointing spur. The lower leaves sheath the stem and are up to 8″ long, oval at the base and pointed at the tip. The upper leaves are smaller and linear.

A large beautiful Orchid, it can be found blooming in mid-summer in damp fields and woods. Although once common in our area, it has now become rather scarce and should be protected. Two similar species are the Small Fringed Orchid *(H. psycodes),* with smaller flowers, and the Purple Fringeless Orchid *(H. peramoena),* with a fringeless lip.

WILD GINGER

Asarum canadense
Birthwort Family

RED/BROWN
April–June
Plate 18

Flower: 1½″ wide; **Plant:** 6–12″ high

Hidden under the leaves of this plant in a crotch formed by 2 leaf stalks is a solitary flower growing at ground level. It is dark red or brownish in color, cup-like and has 3 pointed lobes. The 2 large leaves above the blossom are 3–6″ wide, heart-shaped and have hairy stalks.

Wild Ginger grows in rich woods. The root has a strong ginger-like odor and taste, and can be used as a substitute for ginger.

RED TRILLIUM   RED
Trillium erectum   April–June
Lily Family   Plate 19
Flower: 2½" wide;   **Plant:** 8–16" high

A showy, dull red, ill-scented flower, with 3 petals and
3 sepals, which all flare outward from the base, grows on
a short, reclining stalk above the leaves of this plant. Occasionally a white, green or yellowish variety is seen. Directly below the flower, the leaves are in a whorl of 3 and
are broad, pointed, stalkless, dark green and up to 7"
long.

One of our most common Trilliums, it is found in rich
woods. Other names for it include: Birthwort, Wake-
robin (it blooms before the first robin in the spring), Purple Trillium and Stinking Benjamin.

WILD COLUMBINE   RED-YELLOW
Aquilegia canadensis   April–July
Buttercup Family   Plate 19
Flower: 1–2" long;   **Plant:** 1–2' high

Nodding at the ends of long stems, these red and yellow flowers have long spurs and many protruding yellow
stamens. Long-stalked compound leaves, 4–6" in length,
are divided into 9–27 light green leaflets.

Rocky outcrops and wooded or open slopes are likely
spots to find this flower. Bumblebees, butterflies, moths
and hummingbirds all feed on the nectar contained deep
in the spur. The bumblebee, however, unable to reach
the nectar via the usual route, may bite a hole in the rear
of the spur in order to feed directly. This action thwarts
the mechanism for pollination since the bee does not get
exposed to pollen.

NORTHERN PITCHER PLANT
Sarracenia purpurea
Pitcher Plant Family
Flower: 2″ wide;   **Plant:** 8–24″ high

RED
June–July
Plate 19

Northern Pitcher Plant has large, nodding, deep red, 5-petalled, globular flowers which grow singly on leafless stalks. Surrounding the base of the plant are veined, red or green pitcher-like leaves, 4–12″ long, each with a broad flaring lip lined with downward-pointing hairs which aid in trapping insects.

A unique carnivorous plant, it can be found in sphagnum bogs. The "pitchers" are usually partially filled with water into which insects fall. Unable to climb out over the hairs on the lips of the leaf, the insects drown and are digested by enzymes and bacteria. The nutrients which result from this process, particularly nitrogen compounds, are absorbed by the plant.

CARDINAL FLOWER
Lobelia cardinalis
Bluebell Family
Flower: 1½″ long;   **Plant:** 2–4′ high

RED
July–Sept.
Plate 19

The numerous bright scarlet, tubular, 2-lipped flowers of this plant grow in an elongated cluster on a tall stalk. Long stamens protrude through a split in the upper lip of each blossom. The lower lip is 3-lobed. The dark green leaves are up to 6″ long, alternate, toothed and lance-shaped.

Cardinal Flower grows in moist areas such as wet meadows, swamps and along stream banks. Because of the structure of this plant only the hummingbird is capable of pollinating it. Overpicking has greatly reduced this once common flower of our area.

BLUE COHOSH
Caulophyllum thalictroides
Barberry Family
Flower: ½" wide; **Plant:** 1–3' high

GREEN
April–June
Plate 20

These inconspicuous yellowish-green or bronze-green flowers have 6 pointed sepals, 6 smaller petals and are in a loose terminal cluster. The 2 alternate, compound leaves are divided into many egg-shaped leaflets and are similar to the Meadow Rues *(Thalictrum)* in shape and arrangement.

Blue Cohosh is found in rich deep woods. It produces blue berry-like seeds in a loose terminal cluster on an inflated stalk.

JACK-IN-THE-PULPIT
Arisaema atrorubens
Arum Family
"Jack": 2–3" long; **Plant:** 1–3' high

GREEN
April–June
Plate 20

This plant has a club-like spadix (Jack) enclosed by a tall, green, curving hood or spathe (the pulpit), which is sometimes streaked with brown or purple. The flowers are at the base of the spadix and cannot be seen without destroying the plant. Leaves, usually 2, are taller than the spathe and are divided into 3 dull green, veined leaflets.

Jack-in-the-pulpit is found in damp woods and swamps. It is also called Indian Turnip because the fleshy roots were once cooked and eaten as a vegetable by Indians. If eaten raw it causes a strong burning sensation. Some authorities recognize 3 species of this plant, others group them under one. Only minor differences separate the varieties.

HAIRY SOLOMON'S SEAL
Polygonatum pubescens
Lily Family

GREEN
May–June
Plate 20

Flower: ½–⅔" long;   **Plant:** 8–36" high

Dangling from the leaf axils on the long arching stem of this plant there are usually 2 yellowish-green, bell-like flowers. Alternate leaves, 2–6" long, have parallel veins, are untoothed, stalkless, lance-shaped, light green and have minute hairs along the veins on the undersides.

Look for this common plant in dry or moist woods and thickets. Smooth Solomon's Seal *(P. biflorum)* is very similar but the leaves are smooth on both sides. Great Solomon's Seal *(P. canaliculatum)* is larger, up to 7' tall, and has from 2–10 larger flowers in each cluster. False Solomon's Seal *(Smilacina racemosa)* bears flowers in a long cluster at the tip of the stalk.

INDIAN CUCUMBER ROOT
Medeola virginiana
Lily Family

GREEN
May–July
Plate 20

Flower: ½" long;   **Plant:** 1–2½' high

The several inconspicuous yellowish-green flowers of this plant nod from a stalk that sometimes bends down below the top whorl of leaves. Each flower has 6 reddish, protruding stamens, 3 petals, 3 sepals and 3 brownish, recurved stigmas. Light green, ovate, toothless leaves circle the woolly unbranched stem; 3 at the top, 1–3" long, and 6–10 at the midpoint, 2½–5" long.

Indian Cucumber Root is found in moist woodlands. In the fall, 2–3 dark bluish-purple berries appear and the leaves become an attractive dull crimson. The root was used by the Indians for food, but since the plant is becoming rare it is no longer wise to use it for this purpose.

COLTSFOOT
Tussilago farfara
Sunflower Family

YELLOW
March–June
Plate 21

Flower: head 1″ wide; **Plant:** 3–18″ high

Coltsfoot has a single, dandelion-like yellow flower head made up of thin ray flowers surrounding central disk flowers. Its stalk is covered with scales. The leaves, which do not appear until the plant has bloomed, are 2–7″ long, basal, long-stalked, slightly toothed, and whitish below. Heart-shaped and with a deep cleft at the base, the leaf blade looks somewhat like a colt's foot.

Large patches of this plant can be found in our area. Look for it along roadsides, streams and on wet banks. It is one of the earliest flowers to bloom in the spring. Coltsfoot is reputed to be of value in treating coughs.

MARSH MARIGOLD
Caltha palustris
Buttercup Family

YELLOW
April–June
Plate 21

Flower: 1–1½″ wide; **Plant:** 1–2′ high

A clump of shiny yellow flowers, which resemble large Buttercups, grow on this plant of early spring. The flowers lack petals, have 5–9 petal-like sepals, and numerous stamens and pistils of a darker yellow. Leaves are heart-shaped, waxy and very glossy. The basal ones, 2–7″ wide, are dark green, stalked and slightly toothed or notched; the upper ones are stalkless. The stem of the plant is thick, hollow and branching.

Also called Cowslip, this plant is common in moist places such as swamps, wet meadows and along streams and brooks. The young leaves may be eaten but must be thoroughly boiled in several changes of water.

WILD OATS   YELLOW
Uvularia sessilifolia   April–June
Lily Family   Plate 21
Flower: 1" long; **Plant:** 6–12" high

Shaped like a narrow bell, this small, single, pale yellow flower hangs from the end of a drooping branch. Unstalked, oblong leaves are 1¾–3" long, light green above and paler below. The plant stem is forked near the top.

Large carpets of Wild Oats grow in moist woods and thickets. There are many common names for the plant, among them being Sessile Bellwort and Little Merrybells. Perfoliate Bellwort *(U. perfoliata)*, a related species, has leaves that appear to be pierced by the stem. Large-flowered Bellwort *(U. grandiflora)* has larger, brighter yellow flowers and perfoliate leaves.

BARREN STRAWBERRY   YELLOW
Waldsteinia fragarioides   April–June
Rose Family   Plate 21
Flower: ½" wide; **Plant:** 3–8" high

Several yellow, 5-petalled flowers, each with 5 sepals and numerous stamens, are borne on leafless stalks of this low, Strawberry-like plant. The long-stalked, basal, evergreen leaves are divided into 3 wedge-shaped, toothed leaflets each 1–2" long.

Barren Strawberry grows in woods and clearings. Its fruit is not edible and the plant lacks runners. Indian Strawberry *(Duchesnea indica)*, a trailing plant, has leaflets that are more pointed, flowers that grow singly, and bracts that exceed the petals and sepals in length.

GOLDEN ALEXANDERS
Zizia aurea
Parsley Family

YELLOW
April–June
Plate 22

Flower: cluster 2″ wide; **Plant:** 1–3′ high

This plant has compound umbels made up of flat-topped clusters of tiny, dull yellow-gold flowers. The central flower of each cluster is stalkless. An umbel may have as many as 20 cluster-bearing stalks, all equal in length. Light green, 3-part leaves are again divided into 3–7 narrow, pointed, toothed leaflets. The stem is often tinged with red.

Look for Golden Alexanders in moist woods, meadows, thickets and swamps.

TROUT LILY
Erythronium americanum
Lily Family

YELLOW
April–June
Plate 22

Flower: 1″ wide; **Plant:** 4–10″ high

On a stalk arising from the ground this plant bears a solitary, nodding, lily-like flower, brownish-yellow on the outside and golden yellow inside, with 3 petals and 3 sepals, all reflexed, and 6 conspicuous golden brown stamens. At the base of the stem are 2 pale, grayish-green, purple-mottled leaves, 2–8″ long, smooth, lance-shaped and usually pointing in opposite directions.

Trout Lily grows in large colonies at the borders of moist woods and in thickets. Other common names for it include Fawn Lily, Adder's Tongue and Dogtooth Violet. Trout Lily is an especially appropriate name for the plant since it blooms along brooks at about the time the trout season begins.

CLINTONIA

Clintonia borealis
Lily Family

YELLOW
May–July
Plate 22

Flower: ¾–1″ long;   **Plant:** 6–15″ high

From 3–6 greenish-yellow, lily-like, nodding flowers grow at the top of a long leafless stalk of this plant. Each flower has 3 petals, 3 petal-like sepals and 6 stamens. The 2–3 broad, lance-shaped, shining, dark green, basal leaves, 5–8″ long, resemble the leaves of an Orchid.

Clintonia grows in cool moist woods in acid soil. It attracts great numbers of Yellow Swallowtail butterflies. In mid-summer the pollinated flowers give way to large attractive dark blue berries which are believed to be poisonous. Because of the striking color of the berries, the name Bluebead Lily is also used for this plant. The name Clintonia was given the plant to honor DeWitt Clinton, a former Governor of New York.

ROUGH-FRUITED CINQUEFOIL

Potentilla recta
Rose Family

YELLOW
May–Aug.
Plate 22

Flower: ¾″ wide;   **Plant:** 1–2′ high

This plant has sparse, flat-topped clusters of lemon-yellow flowers with 5 notched petals, 5 sepals, and numerous stamens and pistils. The deep green compound leaves are divided into 5–7 narrow, blunt-tipped, toothed leaflets which are hairy underneath and only slightly so on top.

An erect rough plant, it is very common on roadsides and in dry fields. There are many Cinquefoils, all very similar, with 5 petals which are usually yellow, and 5 sepals which can be seen between the petals. The number of the finger-like leaves may vary but usually there will be 5. The name Cinquefoil is French for "five leaves."

YELLOW GOATSBEARD

Tragopogon pratensis
Sunflower Family
Flower: head 1–2½″ wide; **Plant:** 1–3′ high

YELLOW
May–Aug.
Plate 23

Growing at the top of a long smooth stem, this plant has a single, dandelion-like flower head with many pale yellow rays. Beneath the blossom are long-pointed, green bracts, usually less than 1″ long. Grass-like leaves, up to 1′ long, are broad at the base and have long, narrow, sharp tips.

Yellow Goatsbeard can be found in waste places and along roadsides. The basal leaves are edible, either cooked as a vegetable or raw in a salad. The flower opens in early morning and closes at midday. Seed-like fruits, each with a feathery parachute of bristles, form a conspicuous fluffy globe after the flower has matured.

YELLOW POND LILY

Nuphar variegatum
Water Lily Family
Flower: 1½–2½″ wide; **Plant:** aquatic

YELLOW
May–Sept.
Plate 23

This cup-like, floating yellow flower has 6 fleshy, petal-like sepals and many small yellow petals resembling stamens. The leaves are 3–15″ long, heart-shaped with rounded basal lobes, and they generally float on the water.

Look in ponds and the sluggish water of quiet streams for this very familiar yellow flower. Also called Bullhead Lily, it is our most familiar yellow Pond Lily. Common Spatterdock *(N. advena),* also called Cow Lily, has leaves which are frequently raised above the water.

SWAMP CANDLES

YELLOW

Lysimachia terrestris

June–Aug.

Primrose Family

Plate 23

Flower: ½" wide;　**Plant:** 1–3' high

Small, yellow, star-like flowers, each with 5 petals, 5 stamens and a circle of red dots in the center, are in a terminal spike-like cluster on the erect stem of this plant. Paired leaves are 1½–4" long, lance-shaped and sharp-pointed at both ends. Small reddish bulblets often appear in the leaf axils after the plant has flowered.

Large spectacular displays of Swamp Candles, also called Yellow Loosestrife, are often seen in marshes, moist thickets and on low wet ground, where it spreads rapidly by underground stems.

SUNDROPS

YELLOW

Oenothera fruticosa

June–Aug.

Evening Primrose Family

Plate 23

Flower: ½–1" wide;　**Plant:** 1–3' high

The flowers of this plant, borne in a loose, terminal, drooping cluster, are bright golden yellow with 4 broad petals notched at the tip. A prominent cross-shaped stigma is at the center of the flower. Leaves are narrow, lance-shaped and slightly toothed or toothless. The plant may be erect or branched and spreading.

Sundrops prefer dry or sandy soil and can be found in fields, meadows and along roadsides. Unlike other members of the Evening Primrose family, Sundrops bloom in the daytime. There are many variations within this species.

FRINGED LOOSESTRIFE
Lysimachia ciliata
Primrose Family

YELLOW
June–Aug.
Plate 24

Flower: ¾″ wide; **Plant:** 1–4′ high

Yellow flowers, each with 5 toothed, sharp-pointed, nearly round petals, and 10 stamens, are on long, slender, stalks which arise from the leaf axils of this plant. The flowers usually point outward or downward. The leaves are up to 5″ long, opposite, and oval or lance-shaped.

Fringed Loosestrife is a loosely branched, erect plant found in wet areas. Look for it in damp woods, wet thickets and roadside ditches. The common name for this species refers to the large spreading hairs which fringe the leaf stalk.

BIRDSFOOT TREFOIL
Lotus corniculatus
Pea Family

YELLOW
June–Sept.
Plate 24

Flower: ½″ long; **Plant:** 6–24″ high

Low, often reclining, this plant has bright yellow, pea-like flowers in small flat-topped clusters at the ends of branches. The clover-like leaves have 5 parts, not 3 as the name "Trefoil" implies. There are 3 ovate, entire or slightly toothed leaflets about ½″ long at the upper end of the leaf, and 2 leaflet-like stipules at the base of the leaf stalk.

Birdsfoot Trefoil was introduced from Europe and has become widespread in fields and along roadsides throughout our area. The slender seedpod resembles a bird's foot; hence its common name.

COMMON ST. JOHNSWORT
Hypericum perforatum
St. Johnswort Family
Flower: ¾–1″ wide; **Plant:** 1–2½′ high

YELLOW
June–Sept.
Plate 24

Golden yellow flowers, each with numerous stamens, and 5 petals marked at their margins with black dots, are in a broad, branching cluster at the top of this plant. Small, narrowly oblong leaves, 1–2″, are opposite and have translucent dots as a distinguishing feature.

Common in fields, waste places and along roadsides, it is said to bloom on June 24th, St. John's Eve. Naturalized from Europe, this perennial weedy plant is our most widespread St. Johnswort.

COMMON MULLEIN
Verbascum thapsus
Snapdragon Family
Flower: ¾–1″ wide; **Plant:** 2–6′ high

YELLOW
June–Sept.
Plate 24

Crowded in a long spike-like cluster on a stout, erect, woolly stem, this plant has saucer-shaped, 5-petalled yellow flowers, only a few of which open at a time. There is a basal rosette of thick, velvety, gray-green leaves. These lower leaves are stalked, oblong and up to 12″ long. The upper leaves are smaller, lack stalks, and grow into the stem.

Common Mullein is a very familiar rough weed found along our roadsides and in fields and waste places. The plant has many uses from torches to cures for various ailments such as colds, earaches and inflammations. Indians used to line their moccasins with the leaves to keep out the cold. Because of the woolly leaves, the plant is sometimes called Beggar's Blanket and Flannel Plant.

EVENING PRIMROSE
Oenothera biennis
Evening Primrose Family
Flower: 1–2″ wide;   **Plant:** 2–5′ high

YELLOW
June–Sept.
Plate 25

Clustered at the top of a leafy stalk, this plant has pure yellow, lemon-scented flowers with 4 petals, 4 reflexed sepals, 8 prominent stamens and a cross-shaped stigma. The stem is hairy and usually purple-tinged. Light green leaves, 4–8″ long, are lance-shaped, alternate and slightly toothed.

This common biennial plant is found in dry soils of fields, roadsides and open spaces. Each flower blooms only once, opening at twilight and closing at noon the following day. The roots of the plant are edible, and birds feed on the seeds.

BUTTER-AND-EGGS
Linaria vulgaris
Snapdragon Family
Flower: 1″ long;   **Plant:** 1–3′ high

YELLOW
June–Oct.
Plate 25

The yellow flowers of this plant are in a crowded terminal spike on a leafy stem. Each flower has 2 yellow lips, the upper one 2-lobed, the lower one 3-lobed with orange ridges. A long narrow spur hangs down from the back of each blossom. The numerous bluish-green leaves, 1–2″ long, grow alternately around the stem.

Resembling the familiar garden Snapdragon, this plant is a common sight along roadsides and in waste places. Insects are guided to the nectar in the spur by an orange pathway on the lower lip of the flower. The "butter" referred to in the common name relates to the yellow petals of the flower, the "eggs" to the orange spot on the lower lip. Another name for the plant is Toadflax.

BLACK-EYED SUSAN
Rudbeckia hirta
Sunflower Family

YELLOW
June–Oct.
Plate 25

Flower: head 2–3″ wide; **Plant:** 1–3′ high

Daisy-like blossoms, each with 10–20 showy, golden yellow ray flowers surrounding a dark brown central cone, grow on the rough stems of this familiar plant. The hairy coarse leaves, 2–7″ long, are lance-shaped and alternate. The lower leaves are slightly toothed, or entire, and have 3 prominent veins.

Black-eyed Susan is common in fields, waste places and open meadows. A biennial plant, it forms a rosette of leaves the first year and bears flowers the second year. Indians once used a tea made from the roots to cure colds.

GREEN-HEADED CONEFLOWER
Rudbeckia laciniata
Sunflower Family

YELLOW
July–Sept.
Plate 25

Flower: head 2½–4″ wide; **Plant:** 3–10′ high

Green-headed Coneflower has 6–10 drooping, yellow ray flowers surrounding a greenish-yellow disk which turns brown and elongates at maturity. The leaves are dark green, thin in texture, alternate, smooth and irregularly divided. The lower leaves have 5–7 lobed leaflets and long petioles; the upper leaves have 3–5 segments and may have short petioles or lack petioles entirely. The stems are tall, leafy, branched and smooth.

Also called Tall Coneflower, this plant can be found in swamps, moist thickets and roadside ditches.

GOLDENROD
Solidago spp.
Sunflower Family
Flower: heads ⅛–¼" long;   **Plant:** 2–7' high

YELLOW
July–Oct.
Plate 26

The Goldenrods have showy clusters of small, usually yellow flowers with 3–16 tiny rays surrounding a central disk. The clusters are of various shapes and may contain hundreds of flower heads. The leaves are alternate and either toothed or entire. Perennial, erect plants, they may have a single stalk or be slightly branched.

Found just about everywhere in fields and meadows and along roadsides, the plants are very recognizable and familiar to all. There are about 30 species in New York and it is very difficult to distinguish between them. Botanists separate them by differences in stems, leaves and flowers. Goldenrod has been falsely blamed for causing hayfever for it has been shown that the pollen is too heavy to be carried on the wind, and that Ragweed is actually the guilty plant.

ORANGE HAWKWEED
Hieracium aurantiacum
Sunflower Family
Flower: heads ¾" wide;   **Plant:** 1–2' high

ORANGE
June–Sept.
Plate 26

A small cluster of red-orange flowers are at the top of the hairy stem of this plant. Each flower is made up entirely of ray flowers, finely fringed at the tips. There are no disk flowers. Green bracts around the flower heads are covered with dark gland-tipped hairs. Coarse, blunt, lance-shaped, hairy leaves, 2–5" long, are in a basal rosette.

Hawkweed is common in fields, clearings and along roadsides. It is also known as Devil's Paintbrush because farmers consider it such a troublesome weed. It was once thought that hawks ate the plant to strengthen their vision.

BUTTERFLY WEED

ORANGE
July–Aug.
Plate 26

Asclepias tuberosa
Milkweed Family

Flower: ⅜" wide; **Plant:** 1–2½' high

Butterfly Weed has erect, flat-topped clusters of small, bright orange flowers. Each flower has 5 reflexed petals and a central crown. The clusters are about 2" wide and grow at the top of leafy, hairy stems. The light olive-green leaves, 2–6" long, are alternate, oblong, narrow and pointed. Slender seedpods, borne erect on short stalks, are spindle-shaped.

Look for this showy plant along dry open roadsides and in fields. It is the only member of the Milkweed family with alternate leaves and clear juice. Butterflies are attracted to the brilliant blossoms. Because Indians once chewed the root to cure lung ailments, it is also called Pleurisy Root.

SPOTTED TOUCH-ME-NOT

ORANGE
July–Sept.
Plate 26

Impatiens capensis
Touch-me-not Family

Flower: 1" long; **Plant:** 2–5' high

Dangling at the ends of the long, succulent, translucent stems of this plant are orange, 3-petalled flowers with red-brown spots and a sac-like sepal. From the back of each blossom a long spur curves beneath and parallel to the underside of the flower. The leaves, 1½–3½" long, are alternate, oval and coarsely toothed.

This plant grows abundantly in moist shady places. It is called Touch-me-not because the mature seedpod "explodes" when touched, scattering its contents. The seeds may be eaten, and have a flavor similar to English walnuts. The greens, when not more than 6" high, may be cooked, and sprouts, 2" or less, may be used in salads. The itch of poison ivy may be relieved by applying the juice from the stem. The pretty little blossoms that hang like pendants from the branches may be the reason the plant is called Jewelweed.

MARSH BLUE VIOLET

Viola cucullata
Violet Family

BLUE
April–June
Plate 27

Flower: ½–¾″ wide; **Plant:** 3–8″ high

This Violet has 5 blue petals which are darker toward the throat. The lateral petals are bearded with club-like hairs, and the lower petal is shorter and has dark veins. The flowers are on leafless stems and are taller than the leaves. Heart-shaped leaves are up to 5″ long.

Wet habitats such as springs, bogs and damp meadows are preferred by this plant. The Common Blue Violet *(V. papilionacea)* is a very similar species but it has a longer lower petal with a spur, and all 3 lower petals are strongly veined.

BLUETS

Houstonia caerulea
Bedstraw Family

BLUE
April–July
Plate 27

Flower: ½″ wide; **Plant:** 3–6″ high

Bluets are very tiny, pale blue flowers which grow singly on slender, erect, branching stems. Each flower has a golden yellow center and a tubular corolla with 4 lobes spreading at right angles from the tube. The basal leaves, up to ½″ in length, are oblong and grow in tufts. The leaves of the stem are tiny and opposite.

Large mats of this plant, which prefers acid soil, grow on grassy slopes, roadsides, lawns, and in fields and thickets. Occasionally white-flowered plants are seen. Quaker Ladies and Innocence are other common names by which it is known.

BLUE FLAG
Iris versicolor
Iris Family

BLUE-VIOLET
May–July
Plate 27

Flower: 2¼–4″ wide; **Plant:** 2–3′ high

Growing on the sturdy stalk of this plant, which resembles the garden Iris, are several blue-violet flowers, each with 3 petals and 3 sepals. The sepals, which are not bearded, have dark veins and a whitish spot marked with yellow at the base. The petals are narrower than the sepals and more erect. Arising from a basal cluster and sheathing the flower stem are long, stiff, narrow, grayish-green leaves, ½–1″ wide and up to 32″ long.

Look for this Iris in swamps and wet meadows. Other names for it are Larger Blue Flag and Wild Iris. A similar species, Slender Blue Flag *(I. prismatica)* has very narrow, grass-like leaves less than ¼″ wide.

COW VETCH
Vicia cracca
Pea Family

BLUE/PURPLE
May–Aug.
Plate 27

Flower: ½″ long; **Plant:** vine to 4′ long

These pea-like, tubular, blue or purple flowers grow in dense, 1-sided racemes from stalks, up to 4″ long, which arise from the leaf axils of the plant. Each leaf has a pair of tendrils at the tip and 8–12 pairs of narrow leaflets, 1″ long, arranged opposite one another along the stem.

Cow Vetch is a finely downy, climbing perennial plant which can be found growing profusely in old fields, meadows and along roads. Other names for this species are Blue Vetch and Tufted Vetch.

COMMON SPEEDWELL   BLUE
Veronica officinalis   May–Aug.
Snapdragon Family   Plate 28
Flower: ¼″ wide;   **Plant:** creeper

Small, pale blue flowers grow in long-stalked clusters, 3–10″ high, from the leaf axils of this plant. Each flower has 4 petals, 3 of which are round; the lowest petal is smaller and narrower. There are 2 protruding stamens. The leaves, 2″ long, are opposite, elliptical, and narrow at the base. The plant is hairy and reclining.

This Speedwell is found along banks, and in dry fields and open woods, where it often forms large mats. Bird's-Eye Speedwell or Germander Speedwell *(V. chamaedrys)* is a similar species but has larger flowers, up to ½″ wide, and the leaves are egg-shaped and more coarsely toothed. Common Speedwell is also known as Gypsyweed.

COMMON BLUE-EYED GRASS   BLUE
Sisyrinchium montanum   June–July
Iris Family   Plate 28
Flower: ½–¾″ wide;   **Plant:** 4–20″ high

These deep violet-blue flowers with yellow centers grow singly or in a small cluster on a long, flat, twisted, un-branched stalk. Each flower has 3 petals and 3 sepals, all with pointed tips. The basal leaves, over ¼″ wide and 4–20″ long, are grass-like. A pointed bract extends over each flower head.

A very widespread plant, it is found in fields and meadows. Usually only one flower on a stem blooms at a time, opening in bright sun and lasting but a day. Pointed Blue-eyed Grass *(S. angustifolium)* has narrower leaves, under ¼″, and branched stalks.

HAREBELL BLUE
Campanula rotundifolia June–Sept.
Bluebell Family Plate 28
Flower: ¾″ long; **Plant:** 6–20″ high

Harebell has one or more blue, nodding, bell-like, 5-lobed flowers growing at the tips of wiry, thread-like, much-branched stems. There are numerous linear, pale olive-green leaves, up to 3″ long. Basal leaves, small and broadly ovate, fade before the plant blooms. The base of the stem is sometimes hairy.

This flower can be found everywhere, on rocky banks and slopes, meadows and shores, at high altitudes and at low. A similar species, Creeping Bellflower *(C. rapunculoides)* has flowers which usually grow on only one side of an erect stem. Harebell is also known as Bluebells-of-Scotland.

VIPER'S BUGLOSS BLUE
Echium vulgare June–Sept.
Forget-me-not Family Plate 28
Flower: ¾″ long; **Plant:** 1–2½′ high

This hairy, bristly plant has a showy spike of bright blue tubular flowers, each with 5 red, protruding stamens, and a 5-lobed corolla. The upper lobes of the corolla are longer than the lower ones. One flower opens at a time along the 1-sided, short, curled side branches, which unfold as the flowers bloom. The unstalked leaves are 2–6″ long, very hairy, alternate, oblong, toothless, and grow close to the stem.

Viper's Bugloss, also called Blueweed and Blue Devil, is found along roadsides and in fields and waste places, often in limestone soil. Bugloss (pronounced "bu´-glos") means "ox-tongue" in ancient Greek and refers to the appearance of the leaves.

CHICORY BLUE
Cichorium intybus June–Oct.
Sunflower Family Plate 29
Flower: heads 1–1½″ wide; **Plant:** 1–4′ high

Blue, square-tipped, fringed ray flowers make up the showy heads of this branching plant. The heads are flattish, stalkless and are borne on a stiff stem. Occasionally white or pink flowers are seen. The basal leaves, 3–6″ long, are dandelion-like, oblong or lance-shaped and partly clasping. The stem leaves are smaller.

Chicory is abundant in fields, waste places and along roads. Only a few flowers open at a time and only in bright light. Each lasts a day, fading to pale pink or white as the day lengthens. The roots of the plant are used as a substitute for coffee. The plant is also known as Blue Sailors.

PICKERELWEED BLUE
Pontederia cordata June–Oct.
Pickerelweed Family Plate 29
Flower: ⅓″ long; **Plant:** aquatic

Rising above the water from 1–2′, this aquatic plant bears a dense, showy cluster of violet-blue to purple flowers. The cluster, 3–4″ long, is at the top of a stout stem. The flowers have 2 lips, each with 3 lobes, and 6 stamens, 3 of which protrude. The single, long-stalked leaf, 4–10″ in length, is heart-shaped at the base and tapered at the tip.

Look for Pickerelweed at the edges of lakes, ponds and fresh water marshes. It grows in quiet shallow water such as pickerel prefer, which may account for its common name. The seeds and cooked young leaf stalks are edible. It is also important as a food for deer.

CREEPING BELLFLOWER
Campanula rapunculoides
Bluebell Family
Flower: 1–1½″ long; **Plant:** 1–3′ high

BLUE
July–Sept.
Plate 29

Delicate, nodding bluebells with 5 pointed lobes grow on a long, erect, rigid stem of this plant. Light green lower leaves are heart-shaped and long-stalked. The upper leaves, oval, pointed and alternate, are narrower and short-stalked or stalkless.

Creeping Bellflower is a common garden perennial which has escaped from cultivation and can be found growing wild in fields and along roadsides. Harebell *(C. rotundifolia),* a similar species, has grass-like leaves, thread-like stems, and flowers growing singly or in small clusters at the tops of the stems.

BLUE VERVAIN
Verbena hastata
Vervain Family
Flower: ⅛″ wide; **Plant:** 2–6′ high

BLUE
July–Sept.
Plate 29

Showy, slender spikes of small, tubular flowers with 5 petals branch upward from the top of a square, grooved stem. The flowers bloom a few at a time, advancing up the stalk. Opposite, rough leaves, 4–6″ long, are lance-shaped, short-stalked and coarsely toothed. The lower leaves are sometimes lobed.

Blue Vervain is found in moist meadows, fields, thickets and along roadsides. Both bumblebees and honeybees are especially fond of the plant.

NEW YORK ASTER
Aster novi-belgii
Sunflower Family

BLUE/VIOLET
July–Oct.
Plate 30

Flower: heads 1–1¼″ wide; **Plant:** 8–36″ high

This Aster has numerous heads with 20–40 blue or violet ray flowers surrounding a yellow or reddish central disk. The whitish-green bracts have spreading or backward-curving tips. The leaves, 2–6″ long, are narrowly lance-shaped, smooth, sometimes toothed, and slightly clasp the nearly smooth, slender stem.

Look for this branching plant in meadows, wet spots and along shores and roadsides. There are many Asters and they hybridize quite readily making positive identification very difficult. This one is often mistaken for the New England Aster *(A. novae-angliae)* which has 35–45 ray flowers and a yellowish disk. Its leaves are more crowded and their basal lobes clasp a hairy stem.

BLUE CURLS
Trichostema dichotomum
Mint Family

BLUE
Aug.–Oct.
Plate 30

Flower: ½–¾″ long; **Plant:** 6–30″ high

Blue Curls is a small, delicate plant, generally with 2–3 blue flowers growing at the ends of short branches which arise from the leaf axils. The blossoms have 2 lips and extremely long, curled, violet stamens which protrude in a downward-curving line from the flower cup. The stalkless leaves are opposite, narrow, untoothed, oblong and from ¾–2½″ long. The plant has a woolly-sticky stem, and the leaves are slightly sticky.

Look for this pretty little plant in dry sandy fields. Blue Curls is also called Bastard Pennyroyal because the leaves have an aromatic odor similar to Pennyroyal *Hedeoma* spp.

BLIND GENTIAN
Gentiana clausa
Gentian Family

BLUE
Aug.–Oct.
Plate 30

Flower: 1–1½″ long;   **Plant:** 1–2′ high

Showy, dark blue, bottle-shaped flowers are clustered tightly at the top of the stem and in the axils of the upper leaves of this Gentian. The corollas each have 5 lobes joined together by a whitish, fringed membrane that can only be seen when the flower is forced apart. Ovate, slender-pointed, untoothed leaves, up to 4″ long, are whorled below the clusters and are opposite farther down the stalk.

A very common Gentian, it can be found in moist thickets and wet meadows. The very similar species, Closed or Bottle Gentian *(G. andrewsii)* has fringed membranes which are slightly longer than the corolla lobes and can be seen without opening the tightly closed flower.

FRINGED GENTIAN
Gentiana crinita
Gentian Family

BLUE
Sept.–Oct.
Plate 30

Flower: 2″ long;   Plant: 1–3′ high

Fringed Gentian has violet-blue tubular flowers, each with 4 deeply fringed lobes, borne singly at the ends of erect stems of a branching plant. Yellow-green, oval to lance-shaped leaves, 1–2″ long, have rounded bases, pointed tips, and are opposite and untoothed.

Look for this biennial plant in wet thickets and meadows, and on seepage banks. It opens only in the sun, closes at night, and is one of the last flowers to bloom in the late summer or fall. This beautiful Gentian has become very rare and should never be picked.

INDEX OF COMMON NAMES

References to Pages are for description of flowers, references to Plates are for full-color photographs in Photo Section (pages 33–63).

98

INDEX OF BOTANICAL NAMES

106

ART CREDITS

Flower Drawings by John Mahaffy
Visual Glossary Drawings by Joanne Treffs

FIELD NOTES

FIELD NOTES

FIELD NOTES

FIELD NOTES

FIELD NOTES

FIELD NOTES

FIELD NOTES

FIELD NOTES

FIELD NOTES

FIELD NOTES

FIELD NOTES

FIELD NOTES

FIELD NOTES

FIELD NOTES

FIELD NOTES

FIELD NOTES

FIELD NOTES

FIELD NOTES